Pr
The Witc

"If you're looking to deepen your relationship with your magick, let this be your guide. Filled with a plethora of crafty tips and experiential wisdom, Melanie Marquis ensures that readers get what they've come for: a sense of deeper fulfillment and connection to their spirituality and magick."

—Raven Digitalis, author of
Shadow Magick Compendium

"The *Witch's Bag of Tricks* is a great read. It has an amazing number of those tricks along with good, solid advice and information. Old Witches and new can benefit from this book. I heartily recommend it."

—Raymond Buckland, author of
Buckland's Complete Book of Witchcraft

the
witch's
bag of
tricks

About the Author

Melanie Marquis is a lifelong practitioner of magick. She is the founder of United Witches global coven and the organizer of Denver Pagans. A regular writer for the American Tarot Association and for Llewellyn's popular annuals series, her work has appeared in many publications, including *Pentacle Magazine* and *Circle*. A full-time mother, witch, environmentalist, and writer, she's passionate about finding the mystical in the mundane through personalized magick and practical spirituality.

MELANIE MARQUIS

the
witch's
bag of
tricks

PERSONALIZE YOUR MAGICK & KICKSTART YOUR CRAFT

Llewellyn Publications
Woodbury, Minnesota

Cover design by Kevin R. Brown
Edited by Laura Graves
Ornaments on cover and interior © iStockphoto.com

Llewellyn Publications is a registered trademark of Llewellyn Worldwide Ltd.

ISBN-13: 978-0-7387-2633-5

Llewellyn Worldwide Ltd. does not participate in, endorse, or have any authority or responsibility concerning private business transactions between our authors and the public.

All mail addressed to the author is forwarded but the publisher cannot, unless specifically instructed by the author, give out an address or phone number.

Any Internet references contained in this work are current at publication time, but the publisher cannot guarantee that a specific location will continue to be maintained. Please refer to the publisher's website for links to authors' websites and other sources.

Llewellyn Publications
A Division of Llewellyn Worldwide Ltd.
2143 Wooddale Drive
Woodbury, MN 55125-2989

Printed in the United States of America

Acknowledgments

Thank you, Mr. Carl Weschcke, for inspiring this book to manifest itself as it should be and as it is, through the fact of your own writing being so good that I was led to scrap anything other than my absolute best try.

Special thanks to my family—Andrew, Aidan, and Mia—for the joy and love you bring. Brother Jon, I love you always. And thank you, my extended family, Elizabeth Bridges, Ashley Murphy, Jenny Edwards, Eugene Lumpkin, Tavarius Haynes, Geoff Carr, and the late great Brady Wilkinson, for making my life magickal through your friendship. Thank you, Thoth, for the spider medicine. Thanks also to the dearest Oak Raven for your help and friendship. Nice Punk, thank you for teaching me that shyness can cost the world; I haven't shut up since. To Bill Krause, Elysia Gallo, Laura Graves, Kevin Brown, and all the Llewellyn crew, I am eternally grateful for all your help in making this book a reality. And most of all, thank *you*, for buying this book and reading it.

Dedication

This book is dedicated to my magickal mama, Eva Janice Marquis, for teaching me to believe in magick and for refraining from teaching me dogmatic religion, and to my dad, Charles Marquis, who taught me that writing is an art and that books are important.

Contents

1

Out of the Rut and Into the Fire

When results and returns are less than spectacular, magick begins to lose its luster. We feel ineffective. We wonder what we're doing wrong. We're frustrated and jaded by the fact that something as promising and mysterious as magick can ever become so dull.

Without active pursuit, the mystery fades. Without an ever-increasing stream of nourishment, the soul stops growing. Without challenging exercise and creative application, the psychic faculties that make magick possible falter. We reach a spiritual plateau, and as a result, our magick flatlines.

Whether your rituals have become boring or your spells just aren't working, you don't have to settle for magickal mediocrity. You can improve your magick and make your spellwork more effective. You can get back that spark of excitement and surge of new power you felt when you took your very first steps down your magickal path. The key is just that—we must move forward in order to get there.

Often in established traditions, the route to achieving more advanced magick and heightened spiritual awareness is mapped out through a clear-cut series of steps and lessons. We solitary eclectic practitioners prefer to blaze our own magickal trails, and it's up to us to find our own ways to take our craft further and practice our magick more effectively. We are fully responsible for ourselves, and that responsibility also makes us our own best authorities.

This is not to say that greater spirituality and better magick simply happen on their own. They don't. You need to work for it, push yourself, and dream bigger. It's up to you to set the guidelines and decide how far and how fast you want your magick to grow.

If you're in a magickal rut, get ready to climb out. You don't have to sign on with a specific denomination, join a coven, or commit to another year-and-a-day training program in order to progress. In this book are tips and techniques anyone can use to heighten magickal power, deepen spirituality, sharpen psychic awareness, and more frequently produce magick that works. Let this book be your custom vehicle for traveling further along your own unique path.

Why Magickal Mediocrity Strikes

There are two places in particular along the path where we are likely to get stuck in a rut of magickal mediocrity if we don't actively take steps to climb higher. The first occurs when we reach a point in our development where we've learned all the basics of magick and we're ready to really put it into practice and reap the rewards. We try some spells, but they're only minimally effective. We search for a path that can guide us to better magickal results, but no established branch of Paganism seems to suit us exactly. We look to books, but most are geared toward particular denominations or are too basic. We want to attain greater success with our magick, but if we don't know where to go or how to move forward, we run the risk of going nowhere, settling down in so-so Magickville without any plans or hopes for discovering new territory.

The other time in our lives when we're most prone to digging ourselves into a ditch of magickal boredom and weak spellwork occurs further along the path, when we've been practicing magick for so long that we take it for granted. We cease putting our full will, intent, and consciousness into the process, and our creativity and power reach a standstill. We find ourselves practicing the same less-than-totally satisfying magickal methods we always have, with less enthusiasm and fewer returns each time.

How to Escape It

Attaining deeper spirituality and mastering more advanced magick have two unwavering requirements, and only two. One, you must intend to progress, intend to evolve, intend to take your magick and spirit further than ever. Two, you must actively pursue the next step along the journey. So, what are these next steps? Exactly what skills do we need to acquire to make the plunge into better magick?

Although the paths along your journey are uniquely your own, there are three main roads to progression and development we must pursue if we are to escape magickal mediocrity and avoid spiritual atrophy. We must increase our magickal power, improve our ability to use this power, and truly *own* our power, personalizing our practice to reflect the distinct, unique flavor that we alone can bring to the table to feed the whole of humanity. Let's take a closer look at the three keys to progression that will be explored throughout this book as you embark on your quest to more successful magick.

Increasing Your Power

Without steady development of the components that power the process, magick reaches a point of diminishing returns, where so-so results lead us to apathy, which lead us to more so-so results. By actively developing and improving those skills that are essential to successful spellcasting, we connect ourselves to an everlasting source of magickal power: the thrill of pursuit, the beauty of new discovery, and the joy of evolution.

Through psychic, magickal, and spiritual development, we establish and fortify the consciousness, will, and intent that are the mind, body, and soul of magick. Through expanding our ability to absorb magickal energy, we increase our power potential. By removing blocks to greater progress, we refuse to hold ourselves back.

With more magickal power behind them, magickal actions are much more effective. Whether you simply want to improve your spellcasting or you're striving for magickal mastery, increasing your magickal power will give you a big push in the right direction.

Making Magick More Effective

Magickal power exists for the purpose of using it, not only for everyday, simple things like purifying the vibes in your home, but also for more lofty ambitions like manifesting miracles. But when even typical spells are giving us trouble, producing only minimal effects or failing to function altogether, we lower our expectations of what magick can do. Fantastic magick is possible, but it takes know-how and a strong foundation of confidence to make it happen. Discovering new theories, tools, and techniques can yield better results from any form of magick, and learning how to avoid the mistakes that most often cause magick to fail improves spellcasting ability. Your increasing success will open a new frontier of magickal possibilities!

Owning It

Cookie-cutter magick can only do so much. In order to take things to the next level, we need to design our spells to make optimal use of our own unique power and potential. Whoever you are, you're like no one else, and you can do magick like no one else, too. Each and every one of us is a one-of-a-kind pattern of energies and essence, each with our own affinities, abilities, and purpose. While one-size-fits-all magick can work, you'll get better results if you customize your spellwork to suit you perfectly.

By discovering and honing your unique abilities and designing your magick to make best use of your power, you gain the means for making best use of magick, harnessing its full potential by lending it the skill and style that is yours alone. Exploring your magickal aptitudes and talents and designing your own spells, rituals, and traditions will take the personalization of your practice to more intimate levels, and you'll enjoy more potent and powerful spellcasting as a result.

Put the Spark Back in Spellwork

Making magick that is truly your own, knowing the factors that cause magick to succeed or fail, and steadily increasing your magickal power will lead you further down your own road to more fulfilling, more effective magick. You don't have to take spiritual stagnation and magickal boredom lying down. It's time to stand up and rekindle that fire you felt when you first discovered what magick can do. It's time to get out of the rut and move forward. You've got the compass set to your direction, and you can gain the power to progress along your path further and faster than ever.

Exercise

Chapter exercises are designed to help you reach your own conclusions about the information presented in each section. The only answers to these questions are your own. Consider the following and set your train of thought in motion:

1. Think back to when you took your first steps down the magickal path. What excited you? What intrigued you? What were your doubts?
2. How far are you willing to progress spiritually?
3. To what extent would you like to develop your psychic faculties?
4. What role do consciousness, will, and intent play in magick, and can magick work even if one of these components is not present?

5. What is the best, most ambitious use of magick you can think of?

6. If you were capable of performing such magick, would you?

Taking It Further

We enjoy better results from spellcasting when we learn how to increase our magickal power, use that power most effectively, and fully personalize our practices. What other skills or aspects of development can you think of that would lead to better, more effective magick? What can you do to develop these skills? Choose an aspect of magick to study up on, be it astrology or runecasting, for example, and do so.

In addition to the non-denominational, customizable approach to magickal development offered in this book, research a variety of denomination-based systems for progression, as well. Even if a particular path is not for you, it might still have ideas or techniques from which you can benefit. Strive to go further and take your magick farther, and always keep your eyes open for new vehicles that can get you there.

2

What Magick and We Are Made Of

Even veteran spellcasters benefit from gaining new perspectives on magick. The more ways we have of perceiving reality, the more varied and versatile our magick becomes. One of the things that's so exciting when we first begin to really delve into magick is the joy of discovery as we explore new ideas and expand our concepts. Over time, we come to settle into our ideas, and although those ideas might be perfectly correct, it is the steady pursuit of knowledge on which our awareness and the thrill of magick thrive.

We are unique; each one of us is able to perceive and understand magick and the universe in a way no one else can. Sharing your own ideas and exploring others' perspectives are vital to keep your magickal practice and spiritual journey fresh and exciting. Contemplating, questioning, and communicating about magickal and spiritual philosophy broaden our knowledge and invite us to enjoy brand new views into the heart of magick.

Here we'll explore what magick is, where it comes from, its ultimate purpose, and our role in carrying it out. We'll also take a look at magick's underlying universal principles. Evaluating the theories presented in this chapter will help you clarify, expand, and rejuvenate your own beliefs. While the models and theories offered here provide an effective foundation for understanding and casting powerful magick, there is no substitute for developing and honing your own custom system of magickal philosophy. We listen to others, but we think for ourselves.

Many Models, Many Magicks

Perhaps you think of magick as the ripples of a stone cast into a pond. Maybe you envision and sense magick as a certain everlasting light and love radiating throughout the universe. Perhaps you see magick as an entangled web of traipsing mazes to be traversed and spun. Or maybe you like to think of magick as a cascading style sheet in the web page of life. For every model of magick we can think of, there are at least five million other equally valid ones. Not one of us can currently envision all that is in its entirety, but we each have a unique understanding of certain parts of it. We each have our own ideas for a model of all existence, our most personal beliefs and suspicions about the deepest secrets of magick and the mundane alike.

Our models of magick are ever-expanding works in progress, imperfect and incomplete yet still highly useful in providing a concrete structure for testing theories, improving techniques, and figuring out our own best ways of working powerful magick. Whatever your model of magick might be, the important thing is to have one. Here's mine.

What Magick Is and Where It Comes From

Magick is truly the driving and unifying principle under which the recognized forces that govern matter and energy operate. It is the original action, the flowing current stemming from the universal source. It is the force that separates and weaves together the very fabric of existence. Through consciousness, will, and intent, magickal power is activated.

Let's take a look at an analogy. You can set out some flour and sugar and milk and eggs, but it's not a cake until it's baked. Making a cake requires not only the raw ingredients, but also consciousness, an awareness of what a cake is, and what it is made of. It also takes intent—focused desire—to achieve the result of having created a cake. And it takes will, the active mixing and manipulating of the raw ingredients in a way that is likely to produce a cake. We need not concern ourselves with exactly how the flour particles fuse together with the molecules comprising the milk, or with how the heat of the oven affects the chemical makeup of the sugar. It is as a result of our consciousness, will, and intent that those changes occur. Without them, all you've got is a pile of ingredients. Random chance alone does not a cake make. In order to produce something new and delicious, it takes the power of a baker.

Likewise, it is through consciousness, will, and intent that our diverse universe is shaped and made manifest. It is these three concepts that combine into magickal power, the missing piece of the puzzle, the unrecognized force that is the impetus of change and the underlying structure that makes all that is from all that isn't.

Not Just for Humans

Because consciousness, will, and intent are concepts typically associated with a higher animal mind, we tend to define these forces solely in terms of how they are experienced by advanced mammals like ourselves. However, these processes take place in both living and non-living entities, whether flesh and bone, plant or stone. As people, it is natural for us to personify, that is, attribute to the outside what we know of our own inside. Yet consciousness, will, and intent exist in ways we typically don't acknowledge. They indeed comprise a force that need not be personal or emotional, a force that in fact acts within and throughout everything. This magickal power is the force that puts it all together. It is the mortar that makes its own bricks.

Flip the Switch, Twitch the String

Let's take a look at another analogy. Imagine the universe, everything that exists, as a giant sweater, complete with an intricate pattern of geometric shapes and images, each of us our own little bit of string or part of the decorative pattern. The sweater is essentially one thing: yarn. Yet a sweater is no longer only yarn, although it is comprised of only yarn. The raw material, the yarn, has been twisted and turned, looped upon itself into a specific formation, into a pattern and plan that creates a new entity—a sweater. The knitter knows how to knit, is conscious of what a sweater is, and is aware of its components. The knitter intends to give the yarn a new purpose, a new structure—that of a sweater. The knitter applies will through concrete actions that are likely to achieve the desired result. Like a cake, sweater, or universe, magick cannot be made without consciousness, will, and intent, and the potential of these forces to create change is what we call magickal power. It is the unseen knitter that fashions the yarn into a sweater, it is the switch that turns on the process, the thread we unravel and weave to suit us.

Within, around, and between everything is a place of pure potential, and this potential can be tweaked and twisted through magickal actions to take energy off the default setting and install a new program. Think of it like a mini zero point field that lies within and throughout every single component that comprises the world, a place of potentials waiting to be called into action and manifestation through consciousness, will, and intent.

Magick's Ultimate Purpose

Magick's ultimate purpose, and one of your jobs as a human, is to balance and regulate the energies comprising reality, maintaining the structure while ensuring fluidity. It's like a window screen that keeps out the bugs but lets in the fresh air. It's an uncorked jug that holds liquid but allows you to drink.

Imagining the energies and particles comprising reality as one big river, magick is a way to scoop out a cup full and turn "river" into "glass of water." A glass of water is a glass of water only when the water is contained in a glass—our physical and spiritual bodies, the separations and divisions that house our souls and group molecules into matter, are necessary to maintain the sacred illusion that allows us to perceive reality's infinite diversity. We see not only "river," but a glass of water, a ripple, a rushing current, a floating twig. It is the purpose of magick to maintain and create these divisions while making sure the containers are not unduly sealed so tightly as to shut out all light.

Magickal You: You're Hired!

At the atomic level, our bodies are essentially energy and particles. And yet we know we are more than the flesh we're in. How can nothing more than a mass of quarks and blood and bones weep, love, dream? We are more than the matter we're made of, and that is in fact what makes us matter. Whether you've been the leader of a witches' coven for ten years running, or this is the first occult book you've ever read, you have an inherent ability to perceive and contemplate the cosmic dance of energy, as well as an extraordinary potential to influence the steps of that dance. Through magick, we can free trapped energy and set it to manifest boundless love and light. We can break old patterns and weave new ones. Magick offers us a way to create and a way to destroy. Magick gives purpose to potential, structure to chaos, cords to bind, and a blade to sever.

Where there's love trapped in hate, witches will free it. Where there's light smothered in darkness, witches will banish the haze. Where there is potential without purpose, witches will instruct. Where there is power without direction, witches will put it to good use. Magick is necessary, and it's your job to work it. It's time to extend the scope and enjoy the benefits of your own uniquely specialized occupation.

Universal Principles of Magick

There are of course countless ways to work magick, but throughout cultural and religious differences in methodology, a common thread of universal purpose and principle is woven. Whether a Wiccan calling upon the Crone to turn grief into renewal, a folk magician petitioning mugwort to extract sickness, or a Roma gypsy singing a spell, the basic principles underlying the magick are the same. The magickal power that permeates the Universe, forever creating, transforming, and destroying the material and spiritual containers that temporarily house it, is directed through the magick worker's spiritual actions in order to cause change. Though our techniques and motivations for doing so vary widely, magick's functions and the essentials required to activate those functions are universal to spellcasters everywhere.

Magick's Seven Functions

Just as an infinite variety of songs can be played on a guitar whose one function is making sound, there are unlimited ways in which magick's limited functions can be put to use. Although each of magick's functions can be carried out through a million different methods with a million different results, of all the things magick can do, there are really only seven. It can be used to give purpose, transform, combine, separate, contain, release, and redirect.

Understanding magick's basic functions—knowing exactly what can be done magickally to energy and its components—gives us a technical perspective on the process and allows us to craft more effective and precise magick.

These concepts should seem familiar; although you might not have considered magick from exactly this angle, you have carried out one or more of these seven functions in absolutely every spell you've ever successfully performed. Let's take a closer look at magick's seven functions.

Giving Energy Initial Purpose

Magick can be used to give energy initial purpose, imparting it with an informational code that tells the energy what to do. Just as DNA instructs each cell about how to act, magick informs energy of its purpose. One example is charming an attribute-less glass of water to take on a particular characteristic, such as inducing happiness or calming the nerves. Another example is general energy raising that does not draw power from specific sources—for instance, when power is gathered from the earth at large and given the initial purpose of adding extra force to a spell. Methods for giving energy initial purpose include imparting intent with or without the help of sympathetic or imitative magick.

Transforming Energy

Magick can transform energy, changing its current pattern or coding a new program. Empowering a multi-attributed herb to instead take on a single strong characteristic is one example, such as transforming the healing vibrations in lavender to shift into a romance-inducing vibration. Another example is raising sexual energy and then reprogramming that energy to carry out a defensive charm. Energy can be transformed by infusing it with a stronger energy through intent and methods such as imitative magick and transformation magick.

Combining Energies

Magick can be used to combine energies, fusing one to the other or mixing them together to create something new. Multi-ingredient potions are one example of magickally combining energies. A spell to join a group of people together in a cooperative collaboration is another. Energies can be combined through methods such as imitative and binding magick.

Separating Energies

A cosmic sifter of sorts, magick can separate energies that are fused or mixed together. Curse-breaking, dividing a partnership, or dissolving an alliance are a few examples of magick to separate energies. Methods include using intent to "draw off" one energy from the other, as well as various forms of banishing, imitative, curse-breaking, and severing magick.

Containing Energy

Magick can be used to contain energy, holding it together in a cohesive unit to serve a purpose. Examples include encasing a charm within an object to create a talisman, setting an herb in the sunlight to infuse it with solar energy, and casting the good ol' magick circle. Energy can be contained through methods such as using magickal power to project a field surrounding the energy to be contained, sympathetic magick, binding magick, and transfiguration magick.

Releasing Energy

Magick can be used to release energy, freeing it where it is contained or trapped. Examples include purifying the negative vibes at your office, lifting a curse from an old necklace, and cutting the circle at the end of a rite. Energy can be released by magickal methods such as "drawing out" the energy, opening an exit through which the contained energy can escape, imitative magick, transformation magick, sympathetic magick, banishing, and curse-breaking magick.

Redirecting Energy

Magick can be used to redirect energy, sending it from one level or circuit of reality into another. Examples include a curse that uses the foe's own hate as the binder, a spell to redirect the energy of an addiction into a creative pursuit, or sending the energies of, say, a bay leaf into the universe to promote clairvoyance. Energy can be redirected through pathworking, intent, creating new energy currents, transformation magick, and transfiguration.

Traditional Methods vs. Winging It

If you spend any time in the Pagan community, you're bound to encounter the philosophy that traditions should be strictly adhered to, that the natural magick of an eclectic folk witch is no match for the magick of a person who follows precisely the orthodoxy of a particular spiritual discipline. Traditional methods are relevant and valid—there's undeniable power in the tried and true. But there are other ways of working magick—your ways—that are equally, and often more, effective. When we restrict ourselves to following perfectly laid out traditions precisely, we miss the opportunity to improve those traditions with our own creative ideas and intelligent insights. The limits imposed by our teachers and mentors box us in, and we begin to lose confidence in our own ability to reason out new philosophies and create new modes of magick.

On the other end of the spectrum, if we pull magick out of thin air without any basis whatsoever in fact, theory, practice, or principles, we're not likely to achieve optimal results. What's needed is balance, a mix of old and new, tradition and you. The blueprint of magick is drawn, but that doesn't mean you can't make additions to the plan.

Understanding the universal principles of magick and continuously expanding and improving your own concepts, you can adapt, change, create, and customize methods that are ideally suited and optimally effective for you alone. Your magick is your own; get to know it and play around.

EXERCISE

Contemplating and questioning magickal theories breathes fresh life into our beliefs as well as our spellwork. Ask yourself the following questions about the concepts presented in this chapter.

1. This section outlined seven functions of magick. In what ways have you carried out these functions through your spellwork?
2. Can you think of any additional functions of magick not explored here?
3. What do you feel is magick's ultimate purpose?
4. Do you see similarities in how magick is worked around the world by different practitioners from different cultures? What is the same? What differs?

Taking It Further

Although we recognize that no single model of magick is perfect, it's still beneficial to have a way to visualize and think about the abstract concepts underlying spellwork. Have you developed your own working model of magick? If so, try to expand or improve it. If not, start creating one by jotting down your deepest hunches about existence, reality, and the magickal arts. Seeking out new ideas and actively striving to increase our knowledge makes magick fun and exciting and gives us the motivation and passion to gain greater magickal power.

3

Increasing Your Power Potential

Magickal power, otherwise known as the potential to make magick happen, is directly linked to the quality of the relationship between the spellcaster and the forces worked with in magick. The more open we are to magickal power, the more able we are to absorb it. The more intimately we understand the magickal force, the more magickal power we enjoy. To gain such an understanding and the power that comes with it, we must explore, forging our own friendships with the energies in the world around us. We must also maintain these friendships, as after a while we tend to neglect those relationships we consider given and take for granted.

In fact, experienced witches often get stuck at a plateau and have a more difficult time taking their power to the next level than do beginning witches whose power grows in leaps and bounds. Wherever you are on your path, whether you've cast a million spells or only a few, we've all got to step up in order to progress toward the top—magickal power is your zipline to the apex.

There are many ways to increase your potential for gaining greater magickal power; using a combination of methods is most beneficial. There are things you can do to open your mind and heart. There are exercises you can try to increase your knowledge and understanding of Nature. There are even ways to develop close friendships with deity. Magickal power is essential for successful spellcasting, so don't skimp. Approach the development of your power from all angles, and you'll be rewarded with greater enlightenment and excellent magick skill. By improving our propensity to absorb magickal power, we expand our potential for potent spellcasting. Let's take a look at some ways to do just that.

Open, Not Shut

Put a piece of iron in water, and it will rust. Put a flower in water, and it will grow. Our spirits face a similar fate—cold, closed, and cynical, our souls feel more isolated, more impotent, when we come face to face with true sacred power. On the other hand, if we have an open, warm, and curious attitude, that sacred power will nurture us and support our growth. So how does a scrap of iron turn into a beautiful lotus, anyway? What if we're bitter skeptics at heart—is that something we can stop, or is our spiritual development doomed to only go so far? The answer lies in our willingness to question ourselves. Are past events and emotions preventing us from fully participating in the present? Does cynicism serve us, or does it hold us back?

It's a matter of acknowledging possibility. Sure, there's a possibility that your quest for greater spirituality and magickal power will yield nothing. But there is a much stronger possibility that it *will* yield something, that it will bring you greater understanding, deeper spirituality, and the fulfillment of magickal power increased to its full potential. Acquiring greater magickal power doesn't take blind faith, but it does take an acknowledgment of the possibility that there is more out there, and a hope that discovering more will have some benefits.

Keep an open mind as you proceed on your journey to greater magickal power. Questioning is a positive activity—doing so helps us better define and strengthen our beliefs. Automatically dismissing unfamiliar ideas, however, does not. Try something out before you write it off. Give it a shot. You have nothing to lose, and you have a whole lot of magickal power to gain.

Renew Anew

Long-time spellcrafters who feel their power is not quite what it used to be will benefit from a simple re-dedication rite, renewing the commitment to act as a magickal being striving to progress further into the Mysteries. It's helpful to acknowledge any lapses or oversights in one's personal relationship with the magickal forces. If your magick books have been getting dusty and you haven't worked a spell or taken time to enjoy nature or commune with deity in longer than you can remember, don't gloss over it—face it head on and examine your reasons for being distant. Have you simply been too busy? Did you suffer a major disappointment that caused you to lose faith? How do you plan to remedy this as you move forward to the next level of magickal power? You might not have the answers, but acknowledging the questions is a great way to give your connection with magickal energies a basis of honesty. Once that's out of the way, perform a ceremony of your own design to reestablish your relationship with your favorite sources of magickal power.

If you're fairly new to magick or you don't have any "bad air" to clear with the powers that be, declaring your intentions mentally is often enough to trigger an open state in which you'll be able to soak up more spiritual and magickal knowledge. Simply say, "I'm open to enlightenment. I want answers and I'm willing to seek them. I intend to consider all possibilities that could lead to greater magickal power." If you like, you can add an accompanying ritual, summoning the powers you wish to absorb and inviting those energies to work through your own body.

Self-Immersion Ritual

This ritual is especially helpful for witches whose faith tends to crumble from time to time. Get in a bath and think cynical, bitter, skeptical thoughts. Think of disappointments in your spiritual life, failed spells, feelings of emptiness and isolation, resentments or suspicions of being forsaken or abandoned by deity. Say to yourself, "It's a cruel world. These feelings are valid, but they no longer serve me. I'm letting them go." Feel these energies flowing out of you and into the water.

Now drain the tub completely, rinse it thoroughly, and pour a fresh bath. Get in the water and say to yourself, "It's also a beautiful world. I'm clean and ready; I'm a sponge for spiritual knowledge and I absorb magickal power readily." Think of the water as connected to a greater creative force, a portion of the pure spirit and power that makes magick happen. Feel it around you, seeping into your body. When you get out of the bath, keep this feeling with you, knowing that you are now in a more spiritual state. If you wish, dip a piece of jewelry or another small token into the water to keep as a talisman to remind you of your commitment to magickal possibility.

Greater Exposure, Greater Power—Fast!

We can only increase our magickal power when we're exposed to it: frequent interaction with the sources from which we draw energy for magick is vital. When we spend all day indoors surrounded by our stuff, immersed in our domestic or professional duties with far too little meaningful interaction with other people, and when we only occasionally catch glimpses of the sun and moon, we stay cut off from the very things that can bring us greater magickal power. Mundane life tends to keep us busy—it takes effort to keep a relationship with the magickal world vibrant.

If you find your spells mysteriously waning in power and you've got the time, a daily walk outside is often enough to recharge and reboot the magickal connections upon which your spellwork relies.

Time can be hard come by, though, and for most of us, convenience is not so much a matter of luxury as it is a practical necessity! With a little creative planning, you can integrate regular exposure to magickal energy sources into your daily routine, increasing your magickal power without neglecting your work or sacrificing your free time. Try these quick and easy techniques for upping your exposure to magickal power:

- *Touch it!* Placing your hands flat on the ground, stroking a leaf, holding a stone—touch is your number one medium for absorbing magickal power. Get your hands on nature if only for a second, whether on your way to the office or to the mailbox. Feel the energies flowing into you, sense the nuances of essence, and let some of your own energy flow back into the earth in exchange. If you're homebound, open a window and breathe in the air, or do a similar touching exercise with houseplants.

- *Oust the hermit!* Meaningful and friendly interaction with other people also keeps us connected to magickal power, as every single person on earth has a share of it within them! When you talk to someone, be it the clerk at the grocery store, your daughter, or your boss, strive to make a real connection, truly listening to the other person and tuning in to the energies of his or her core being. Likewise, give others the real you: take off any social masks and speak with authenticity and genuine compassion. When we keep to ourselves, we're restricted to only what lies within ourselves, and our potential for magickal power remains rigid. When we make and enjoy genuine connections with other people, we benefit from a fluid and dynamic exchange of magickal energy that boosts the power of all involved.

- *Get friendly with the force!* Another quick way to increase your power potential is to get to know on a friendly basis the deities or forces you typically work with magickally. Let's face it— every single one of us has something to say and no one to say it to; something to rant about or secret glories and embarrassing moments we don't want to share with even our dearest friends.

You can always trust your gods to keep a secret, though, and talking with your deities or to the higher powers within you in the same way you would talk to a close pal forges a powerful friendship that will lend tremendous strength to your magick. Shoot off an email to Cernunnos care of your own email address, draft a text message to Isis, mutter under your breath to Aphrodite about the attractive stranger you see at the coffee shop, for example. Think of the forces you believe in as personal private friends, and treat them naturally. Expand the scope of your relationship with higher sources of magickal power so your interactions with these forces is not all business—it'll put that power on your side and in your soul.

- *Study up!* Watch a nature documentary while you fold laundry, listen to a recording of genuine rain forest sounds while you exercise, read an environmental magazine while standing in line at the bank or riding the bus to work. Educating yourself about the natural world doesn't have to be time consuming in order to be beneficial. When we are thinking about something, we are directly connected to the energy of that something, and when the something is nature, we find our magickal power rises when we allow it a share of mind. Learning more about nature topics that interest you will deepen your understanding of the natural world and fortify your connection to it, making it easy for your mind and spirit to soak up magickal power like a sponge.

- *Keep it clean!* Just as a mistreated lover can only be pushed so far before walking out on a relationship, angering nature deities by disrespecting the earth might get you blacklisted from accessing that particular power source. Picking up trash when you see it, never littering, and reducing your consumption of natural resources are effective ways to ensure your relationship with the earth and its powers has the trust needed to stay healthy and functional. When you pick up an empty soda bottle in the park or decide to skip the chemical pesticides in your garden, you are lending your energy to the earth and its forces, and the power you give will be returned in greater abundance.

Avoid to Increase

There are additional techniques you can try that will increase your propensity to absorb magickal power. If you really want to reach your full potential, you need to minimize the effects of anything that gets in the way. Consider adopting some or all of these guidelines to greater power:

Minimize Meat Consumption

As every witch knows, our energetic exchanges with the forces of nature can have quite a sway on our magick's power, and eating an over abundance of factory-produced meat can make spells sluggish. Of course, dietary needs and philosophical sensibilities vary, and not everyone is meant to be a vegetarian. The choice of whether or not to partake in meat consumption should be based on your own physical needs and personal beliefs. Whatever you decide is right for you personally, just be sure it's a consciously made, logical decision, something you have put some thought into.

You might find it helpful to examine separately the general idea of meat eating and the modern realities of the commercial meat industry. For most of us, long gone are the days of standing face to face with an animal and deciding consciously to end its life for our own survival. Today, we go to the grocery store, we go to restaurants, and we enjoy our dead animal flesh conveniently placed before us on foam trays or in waxed paper wrappings that disguise all traces of the meal's true origins. The way most of us obtain meat today is far removed from the practice of respectfully hunting animals in the wild. Many animals raised for slaughter are caged, abused, and thrown by the dozens into seldom washed meat grinders for processing. We can probably agree that supporting cruelty to animals does not bring anyone closer to nature. It can certainly inhibit one's ability to absorb magickal power, making our bodies sluggish and leaving us with less energy to devote to magick. A better choice for meat-eaters is to buy from local farmers who are ethical in the treatment of their livestock and who raise their animals without cages or artificial hormones.

Many witches forego meat altogether and choose a vegetarian diet, feeling that it produces a more energized body, mind, and spirit in tune with nature.

If you decide to go vegetarian, you might find that old habits are hard to break, and the thought of giving up meat altogether might be overwhelming. However, cutting back even a little, especially on commercially produced meat, will make you more apt to absorb greater magickal power. If you usually eat meat at every meal, start by having meat only once a day. After that, reduce meat consumption to only a few days a week, gradually cutting back until you're eventually enjoying the benefits of an entirely meat-free diet.

There are many commercially available tasty meat substitutes to help you make the transition and still get the protein and flavors your body craves—it's even possible to make an entirely vegetarian bacon burger! Keep in mind, however, that not all meat substitutes are healthy. It's important to know the origins of our food, be it from the ground or from the flesh. Strive to buy locally whenever possible; supporting local farmer's markets, co-ops, and small "Mom and Pop" grocers offers a sense of connection to your community, and in many cases, much healthier food options to choose from. Find out what commercial meat processing and the global food industry really entails, ask your doctor about your personal dietary needs, and make a conscious choice.

Keep Vices in Check

We all have our vices; escapism is very human! But when we become obsessed or greedy, those escapes turn into cages. Whether it's smoking twenty cigarettes a day, doing every crossword puzzle you can get your hands on, or pining night and day for that long-lost favorite lover—if not kept in check, our vices control us. If you're serious about gaining more magickal power, now is the time to face those addictions and obsessions and decide how much energy you're willing to devote to your vices. A little escapism now and then won't hurt anybody, but fully immersing yourself 24/7 in your chosen obsessions will.

Be aware of the time you spend enjoying your vices. How many minutes or hours a day does your obsession require? Would you rather use that time for something else, like attaining more magickal power? Consciously making these choices is often enough to keep our vices from getting in the way of spiritual and magickal development.

Realize, however, that not all vices are so easily controlled. There's no way to "cut back" on smoking crack, no way to casually decide to use less heroin. Strong addictions like this require commitment to a complete treatment program. The good news is that magick can help you get through the process of overcoming addictions, even very powerful and dangerous ones. See the next chapter for details about magickally overcoming addictions and removing other blocks to greater power.

Don't Let Your Brain Atrophy

An active mind is an absorbent mind, and keeping mental faculties sharp and alert through frequent exercise will make you much more able to absorb magickal power. Read a variety of books. Exercise your psychic abilities. Play thinking games. Ask questions. Seek answers. Learn a new interesting fact every day. Such activities put our minds in a state of learning. Studying random things like the habits of chimps, how to find the square root of a derivative, or how to make sesame tofu, for instance, will transfer over into greater ability to learn and comprehend the lessons of magick and spirit. Keep your mind sharp and active, and you'll be open to receiving more magickal power.

Feeding the Fire

Magickal power is the very stuff magick is made of, and without enough of it, spells lag. Being open to magickal power and actively seeking exposure to such power through practical methods you can work into your daily routines is a surefire way to keep your energy supplies flowing and help your spells pack a punch. Decide for yourself how powerful you want your magick to be, and do everything you can to increase your potential to get there.

EXERCISE

1. Has there ever been a time in your life when you felt your magickal power was at a low point? What caused it? Could you have taken measures to prevent it?

2. What are some places or activities that help you feel totally charged up and full of magickal power?

3. What are your favorite sources of magickal energy to draw on when working magick? Are there other sources you'd like to try?

4. What one quick thing will you do today to increase your exposure to magickal power? What's a lengthier exercise you could try?

Taking It Further

When we increase our potential for attaining magickal power, we are much more likely to be able to access and utilize the amount of energy needed to make spells work and we are far less likely to experience the frustration of weak magick. Why do you think magickal power is important to the magickal process? Do you think a spell has a greater chance for success the more energy it has behind it? Just how much power is needed to make a spell work properly? Contemplate the meaning of magickal power and its relationship to magick and create your own definition. See if you can think of three things to do each day to increase your magickal power. Push yourself to be as magickally powerful as you can possibly be, search out new ways to increase your power, and be open to working with alternate sources of energy. You'll keep your spellwork from becoming stagnant, and you'll stir up fresh fire in your spirit, taking you back to the surge of power you felt when you first discovered your own magickal force.

4

Removing Blocks to Greater Power

As we progress along our magickal path, we sometimes find ourselves brought to a screeching halt. Past pains, current vices, fears, and future doubts can block the road forward and prevent further magickal and spiritual development. Delays happen to all of us at one time or another, no matter how great our skill in the magickal arts or how long we've been in the Craft. Everyone reaches a standstill in their magickal and spiritual development occasionally, and it's nothing to feel ashamed of. In fact, when you're feeling uncomfortable or dissatisfied spiritually, it's a sign that you're ready to progress and that you're strong and spiritually aware enough to face the real challenge of breaking down your current barriers. When we find ourselves having difficulty moving forward, it's time to examine what is holding us back. With the motivation and the methods, we can kick our limits to the curb and move ahead toward greater magickal power. Let's get started.

Suppression, Addiction, and Freeing Trapped Energy

So many of us are survivors and silent bearers of great pain. Whether it is the fear that comes with growing up in the midst of domestic violence, feelings of violation and shame that accompany sexual abuse, or the bottomless sorrow left by the death of someone close, these deepest, most uncomfortable emotions are often locked away for sheer survival. While doing so is a valid and temporarily effective coping mechanism, those trapped feelings are taking up valuable energetic real estate that could otherwise be filled with magickal power. If you don't evict what's trapped, it will eventually take over and bring down the whole neighborhood.

When we are enduring terrible things, the traps of fear, depression, and oppression often imprison our energy. We survive such experiences by doing the imprisoning ourselves, closing off and shielding our spirits so that we cannot be overcome completely by pain. We direct our suffering to a dark, hidden alcove of our mind and think of it as contained, tiny, and managed. Most of our energy is focused inward, bent on being stronger than the cause of suffering and aggressively suppressing our pain, much like a wrestler pinning down an opponent.

In this way we learn to be strong and exert power, and our sense of personal strength becomes inextricably linked to and dependent upon having a source of pain from which to draw that strength. We develop the idea that having power means managing pain, and many of us learn to self-inflict that pain. Some of us suffer by isolating ourselves from other people and living only a faded half-life of who we really are. Others harbor anger or insecurities, or develop a knack for attracting drama.

Still others among us abuse ourselves with drugs, finding the world full of dangerous delights well suited to the purpose of supplying a steady source of pain to (mis)manage. While it can be argued that occasionally altering one's consciousness with certain psychoactive plants is a natural human tendency, addiction is of an entirely different nature. Overusing dangerous drugs or alcohol provides us with a fresh supply of pain as well as a means to suppress it, and our addictions become a source of false security and mock normalcy, giving us a sense of control over our suffering.

The thing to remember is that pain is pain and suffering is suffering—whether from an outside source or self-inflicted, it has the same vibrational pattern and the same basic effects on the spirit. It is an energy of oppression and control, and when we focus all our force on suppressing pain, we are not overcoming it, but feeding into it, allowing it to control and direct more of our energy and become even stronger. As a result, we're closed off to further magickal progress, and our power, far from growing, goes to waste.

This trap can be escaped. It's a matter of overcoming fear and unlocking the door that separates you from your pain, stepping out and reclaiming the part of your force that has been held hostage by suffering or addiction. We must cease directing our energy inward in suppression of pain and instead direct it outward in the creation of contentment and positive change. You expel darkness from a room by turning on a light, not by adding thicker curtains.

Rituals to Reclaim Your Power

Some of us deal with pain or trauma by suppressing it and trying our best to block out those memories and emotions, inadvertently blocking our potential for spiritual growth as we do so. Pain suppression can help us get through in the present and give the tenacity to keep going, but the unbreakable law of suppressed emotions is that if you don't deal with them on your terms, they will eventually deal with you on theirs. Suppressed energies have a way of working their way to the surface subtly at first, manifesting as insecurity, general doubt, or a tendency toward self-oppression that causes us to avoid going after our biggest dreams. Eventually, we crack, and all that negative pent-up emotion comes out swinging, often causing erratic behavior or severe depression that can send us into a whirlwind of self-destruction.

It's much better to deal with difficult memories and emotions actively, on our own schedule, before they erupt in the ugliest of fashions, and in the most inconvenient times and places.

Consulting with counselors, support groups, or mental health professionals can be helpful in many situations. Trying your hand at a new means of expression such as art, music, writing, or an unfamiliar mode of magick can also provide motivation and incite new interest in living life. Ritual work can also help free trapped energies and emotions and clear those out to make room for greater magickal power. Try the magick below to help reclaim your magickal and spiritual strength:

Erode It Away Ritual

This ritual helps release and neutralize trapped emotion. Lay flat on the ground face-down, naked. Obviously, you'll need to find a private and safe place to do this—seriously, it is not at all a good idea to go skyclad in a semi-private area where nosy neighbors or random creeps can see you. If you plan to go out in the woods or to another natural area not on your own property, have a friend with you if possible or at least tell someone exactly where you are and when to expect you back. If there isn't a place outside where you can be safely naked, just do the ritual in your house with the window (but not the blinds!) open, surrounded by houseplants, stones, or other natural things to bring the wild indoors.

Delve into your suppressed memories and painful emotions, feel those energies and sense their vibration. Now sense the energies of the dirt (or the ground below the floor) beneath you; feel its stabilizing force, hone in on its neutrality.

Consciously pull the energy of the earth up into your body, drawing it directly toward your flow of emotion. Let the vibration of the earth energy take prominence and feel the current of your suppressed energies change, becoming neutral and stable. Now direct the flow of energy back into the ground, sending with it as much of your own energy and emotion as possible.

When you feel completely drained, take a few deep breaths and stand up, looking at the place where your body just lay. Now take a pitcher of water and pour it over the area, washing away the top layer of dirt as well as cleansing away the shell in which you had trapped your emotions for so long. If you're doing this ritual indoors, just use a broom to quickly sweep away the stale energy. Express your gratitude.

Lunar/Solar Gateway Ritual

This ritual creates an opening or gateway through which trapped energy can escape. Stand outside in bright sunlight. Get in touch with your trapped energy as much as you can, envisioning it as a dark ball inside you. Feel the solar energy stream into your chest directly toward the dark ball of trapped energy. Visualize the sunlight creating a hole in the ball, and use your intent and consciousness to make the solar energy literally pierce through the trapped energy, creating a tear in the dark ball. Leave it at that and go about your daily business.

That night, stand outside in the moonlight and get in touch with the now-torn dark ball of energy within you. Feel the energies of the moonlight and let it soothe you. Let the energy in the dark ball flow out and up to the moon; visualize the ball deflating as the energy escapes. Absorb the lunar energy into you, letting it flow throughout your body bringing a calm solace and healing. The next day, stand out in the sunlight again and again feel the solar rays stream into your body, this time envisioning the solar energy infusing you with fresh magickal power, filling up the place where the dark ball used to be with a new light. Say thanks to the energies that helped you.

Digest It Ritual

This ritual helps give you the upper hand over trapped emotional energies. Take a whole orange and write on its peel a name or phrase describing your trapped energy. For example, you might write, "abused" or "heartbroken." Write as much as you like, naming names, emotions, dates, whatever suits you.

Hold the orange in your hand and give it your best stern, authoritative look. In your own words, let the orange and the trapped energy it now represents know who's boss. You might say something like, "I've had it with you! I'm eating you and then you'll be processed and done with!"

Peel the orange with determination and strength, casting aside each piece in disgust. Feel powerful—like you're ready to kick some ass! Eat the orange viciously, destroying it with your courageous self. Let nature take its course; your body will digest the food and help you process some of those previously trapped emotions that were blocking you from progressing further. You'll know you're stronger than the pain you've felt. You'll be able to begin letting go of it and start grabbing on to positive energies instead.

Spells to Aid in Overcoming Addictions

The following spells are designed to aid in shifting energy patterns to make taking the first steps out of a painful addiction a little easier. Total recovery requires time, patience, and unpleasantness; there is no magick that will stop physical and emotional symptoms of withdrawal from drugs like alcohol or heroin. These effects must be endured until they run their course. Many find detoxification programs or support groups such as Alcoholics Anonymous or Narcotics Anonymous to be vitally important sources of help and information needed to get through withdrawal, but the work is ultimately that of the individual striving to overcome the addiction. With desire, logic, and willpower, escaping forever the trap of addiction is possible, freeing a tremendous amount of energy and spirit that can then be enjoyed and used to make magick. Check your phone book or the Internet for recovery programs and resources, and try these spells for extra help.

Melt Away Method

Hold an unlit candle with both hands and fall deeply into your craving for your vice of choice. Explore this feeling and discover its many aspects, experiencing how you want the drug physically, emotionally, and mentally. When the craving is most intense, transfer this energy into the candle. Consciously imagine your craving as a dark colored light concentrated in your hands, and then visualize blasting this energy into the candle.

The candle now becomes an outward symbol of your addiction, and you have the power to melt it away. Light the wick and watch the candle shrink. See how the powerful energy of your craving is easily transformed when light is applied to it. Breathe deeply and calmly as you watch the candle melt down. Let the candle melt down completely.

Tear It Up Trick

Find a time when you can be by yourself and write about everything that has caused or continues to cause you pain or sadness. Write freely and deeply, knowing it will be destroyed when you are finished, and that it will not be read by anyone else. Write about your addiction and how it truly makes you feel. Include your suspicions about why you turn to your drug of choice. Confess your deepest fears and your darkest actions.

Read over what you have written and then crumple the paper up tightly. Tear it into pieces to place in an ashtray or other fireproof dish. Set it on fire and burn it to ash. Scatter the ash outside, and know that you have shed a lot of baggage and loosened the chains of your addiction. Do something fun or constructive to put the magick out of your mind.

Something for Nothing Charm

This charm allows you to experience a measure of the feeling a certain drug gives you without actually taking the substance. Sit or stand in the same position you're usually in when using the drug. Think of the feeling you wish to conjure. Align your own energy with this vibration and envision a golden light shining from your forehead. Say, "I am open to all positive energies of this vibration. Please help me to feel this part of the creation in a new and healthy form. So will it be."

Challenging Doubts

Doubt is a major block that can prevent you from increasing your magickal power. When we doubt our own power or abilities, or when we doubt the power and abilities of magick, we are prevented from attaining greater power until we learn to acknowledge and make the most of the power we *do* have. It's like a little kid asking for a new toy when he already has hundreds he doesn't appreciate. If we don't believe in and use to the fullest our personal gifts—magickal or otherwise—we're not likely to acquire any new gifts.

Doubt is a healthy emotion that can trigger questioning and contemplation. Once we've questioned and contemplated, though, it's time to move on and not let unfounded disbelief ruin our chances for success! If you doubt yourself or you doubt what magick can do, don't let this be a block to greater power. Challenge that doubt and put it to the test; suspend it until you see if it's still standing after your experiments. Here are two exercises you can try to help you evaluate if your doubt is reasonable or if it's time to banish it for good.

Doubting Yourself Test

Is there something you wish you could do but just know that you can't? How are you so certain it isn't possible? Try it out; give it a go! First, make a list of your doubts and beside each one, write the reasons why you believe this. Read over your list, pretending that your best friend just wrote it and handed it to you.

Do any of the doubts seem unreasonable, or even downright stupid? Cross them off immediately. What's left? Are these doubts absolutely justified, or is there a chance they're unfounded blocks to greater power? Would it be safe for you to attempt to challenge these doubts? (For instance, you obviously don't want to challenge your doubt of the safety of playing in the middle of the street!)

Now write down one little step you could take to challenge each remaining doubt, a concrete action to put that doubt to the test and give yourself a chance to prove you won't let doubt hold you back. Uncertainty plagues us all, but realize you have a responsibility to yourself and to humanity to do what you know you are meant to do *despite* any doubt. Now go for it, take those steps and see what happens!

Magickal Doubt Destroyer

Have you lost confidence in magick? Do you doubt its power to create real change? Well, test it out, trying simple charms and spells to boost your belief. Keep track of your experiments and the results yielded for a full month, doing a different little something each day to test out the power of magick.

Choose magickal goals that are measurable, so that you'll definitely know when it works. Even simple psychic power exercises like trying to get the wind to change directions or encouraging a stray cat to lick its paw at your telepathic command are beneficial in blasting through magickal doubt. Agree to yourself to suspend doubt as you try each bit of magick; if you don't, it won't stand a chance!

Wait until you have compiled the magickal results for the full month before you make any evaluations. What worked? What didn't? Were any of your doubts proved wrong? If so, knock down the walls and clear the rubble, trying even grander spells that further challenge those past doubts. You'll find your magickal power and skill increase dramatically.

Facing Fears

Sometimes we let fear hold us back from magickal and spiritual progression. Perhaps it's a phobia that makes you feel like a scared, helpless creature, not courageous enough to grow into a full-on super being. In other cases, the fear might stem from a very real and present danger, physically keeping you trapped in a situation where you are unable to be your real self.

Whatever the circumstance, if you're living in fear, it will hold you back. If you are truly committed to being the best you can be and to following your path to the highest heights of magick and spirit, removing the roadblock of fear is imperative.

Spells can help, but safety is first. If you're facing a fear that could lead to your getting hurt, for instance facing a fear of heights by climbing a dangerous mountainside or facing the fear of leaving a violent spouse, don't go it alone! Get some friends to join you, call the police, call a help line—whatever the situation calls for to ensure your personal safety as you face your fear. Try this spell before you face the fear physically.

Fearless Image Spell

This spell can help you gain the belief in yourself you need to successfully face your fear. Draw on a piece of paper an image of yourself bravely overcoming your fear. Make it specific to your own situation, be it a drawing of yourself walking hand in hand with a creepy clown or stomping on your abuser.

Write above the image, "I can do it. I will do it." Sprinkle the image with some courage-enhancing cinnamon, and feel yourself swell with bravery. If you don't feel it, fake it. Puff out your chest and put your chin up. Say out loud that you are strong and brave and that you can easily overtake the fear represented in the image. Destroy the paper by crumpling it up and then ripping it to pieces. Discard the pieces away from your house in a public trash bin, saying as you do so, "I am done with you!" Now take the necessary steps to physically face your fear head on.

Remove the Block and Move Forward

Know that delays, detours, and obstacles along your path can be catalysts for growth. When we feel stuck or like our energy is blocked, we can actively take steps to clear the way forward. As soon as the road can be traversed once more, do so. Seek out new magickal information and experiment with unusual techniques. Explore your spirituality, and strive to go further in your development than you've ever gone before. There are plenty of ills in the world to block and bind us; we are here to overcome them through magickal power.

Answer these questions to discover and challenge what might be blocking you from attaining greater magickal power.

1. Into what do you pour your personal energy? Are you devoting yourself to anything unhealthy?
2. What is the most painful or saddening experience you've ever endured? Are your feelings still intense when you think of it?
3. What do you doubt you can do? What's the worst thing that could happen if you tried? What's the best thing that could happen?
4. What do you fear? What will need to happen in order for you to be prepared to face this fear? What will you do once this fear is conquered?

Taking It Further

It's true that knowledge is power, and when it comes to removing blocks in your path of spiritual and magickal development, knowledge is indispensable! Take some time to learn more about whatever it is that's trapping your energy. Are you hoping to quit smoking? Study up on cigarette manufacturing and the effects of nicotine on the body. Are you ready to heal from childhood sexual abuse? Research the psychological impacts of such abuse and share stories and information with others who have suffered. Are you full of doubt about your musical ability, but you really want to be a rock star? Find out about the music industry and discover how other musicians faced their fears and made it. Whatever is blocking your energy, are you ready to use the techniques in this chapter and your own ideas to remove those blocks? Get to it and embrace the next steps forward!

5

Discovering Affinities

From numbers to elements, from plants to gods, we each have our own preferences and affinities, and learning how to make the most of your unique magickal potential will make your spellwork more successful and will help you discover your own magickal style. This chapter will enable you to understand more about your magickal affinities, and you'll be empowered with knowledge you can harness. Let's do it!

What's Your Element?

Many of us work with all the elements in our magick, summoning earth, air, fire, and water for each and every spell. It makes sense to know the magickal forces equally and to make our magick mimic this natural balance. Still, it's helpful to know exactly which of the elements you're *most* in tune with and why, as you can use this knowledge whenever you want to give a spell an extra boost of intensity or a big splash of your own strong and radiant essence. If water is your element, for example, try emphasizing it throughout the magickal process and making it the primary power source for your spell. This will produce better results than will drawing from all the elements equally or using only an element that doesn't jibe with your soul. Likewise, if you're a fire type, you might not have much luck with water charms, but your candle magick will be ultra-effective.

Do you know your element? Chances are, you either feel very strongly about your primary elemental affinity, or you at least have a notion or a hunch as to what it might be. Exploring these bonds further offers insight into our attractions, which in turn helps us know ourselves better as we refine our special niche in the magickal arts and make our spells more effective through personalized tailoring. We might also discover secondary elemental affinities we can use to our advantage. Here's an activity, a quick survey, and a quiz to try; see what you find!

Winning Element Activity

This activity will help you discover which elements serve you best. Pick a general spell goal, something not strongly associated with any one of the elements. For instance, a spell to improve communication wouldn't be a fair choice because air would have the advantage. At the same time, you'll want a goal that is measurable, so you'll know for certain whether or not the spell succeeded.

Natural growth is one fitting topic your magick could take, as a plant's development depends on all the elements in equal measure. A plant needs fire from the sun, earth from the dirt, water from the clouds, and air to blow those clouds around and scatter the plant's seeds over the earth.

You'll need four seeds of the same variety for your experiment. Choose seeds that have fairly neutral energies. Butter beans, lima beans, or garbanzo beans (chickpeas) are good choices. Plant the beans in individual containers, one bean in each pot. Assign an element to each plant, and label it in some way in case they get rearranged. Every day, invoke each plant's element into it, calling on the air and asking it to help the air plant thrive, summoning the earth to help the earth plant thrive, and so on. Keep all other conditions controlled, ensuring all four plants get equal light and water. Which element's plant sprouts first? After a month, which plant is doing the worst? Which looks healthiest? Which is tallest? The answers will clue you in on your strongest elemental affinities.

Elemental Affinities Survey

Quick! Think of one word to describe each element. Write them down. Then comment on each element in greater detail, writing down anything that comes to mind. You might describe how the element makes you feel, the essence of its energy, or even what kind of music would best represent it. It need not be poetic—just a brainstorming session to help you dig up your deepest notions about the forces of nature.

When you're done, read over it. Did you gush praise for one element, but downplay another? Did you have lots to say about fire, but were pressed for ways to describe air, for example? You'll be able to see and understand more clearly what your heart holds dear.

Quiz: Elemental Instincts

Take this quiz to help identify your most instinctual elemental affinities. Don't think about your answers too much—the first hunch rarely lies.

1. Would you rather:
   A. Feel the wind on your face
   B. Lie down on the forest floor
   C. Stand in the ocean
   D. Sit by a campfire

2. In magick, I'm most drawn to:
   A. Wand work or word charms
   B. Herb magick

C. Potion making

D. Candle magick

3. When I'm upset, it calms me to:

    A. Take slow, deep breaths

    B. Go on a nature hike

    C. Take a bath or shower

    D. Meditate on a candle flame

4. The natural disaster I find most awe-inspiring is:

    A. Tornado

    B. Earthquake

    C. Tidal wave

    D. Wildfire

5. If I could transform at will into one of these animals, I'd choose to be a:

    A. Bird or bat

    B. Forest-dwelling mammal

    C. Sea creature

    D. Reptile or salamander

6. If I were to spend an afternoon playing like a little kid, I would probably:

    A. Fly a kite

    B. Dig in the dirt

    C. Splash around in a pool

    D. Play with sparklers or other small fireworks

7. When I admire a tree, I most appreciate:

    A. The fluttering of the leaves

    B. Its tenacity

    C. Its vitality

    D. Its beauty

8. If I had to choose, I'd rather be:

    A. Caught outside in heavy winds

    B. Covered head to toe in mud

C. Outside in a rainstorm

D. In a desert in scorching heat

9. If I could travel in style, I'd go by:

A. Private jet

B. Limousine

C. Yacht

D. Race car

10. If I won a trip to Hawaii, I'd be most excited about:

A. Parasailing

B. Wandering in the rainforests

C. Enjoying the beach and ocean

D. Exploring the volcanoes

Scoring: mostly As = air, mostly Bs = earth, mostly Cs = water, mostly Ds = fire. Which did you get? Did more than one element tie? Follow up with further exploration and inquiry.

Further Elemental Affinities Exploration

Now it's time to delve deeper. Explore the element or elements indicated as your best match in these activities. If it's water, sit by a stream for awhile, take a bath, stand in the rain. If fire seems to be the one, surround yourself with candles or sit by a campfire. If it's air, take a stroll on a windy day. If it's earth, dig in the dirt or simply lie on the bare ground.

Whichever element you're exploring, immerse yourself in it and try to absorb the element's power into your body, visualizing and willing it to flow into you. Raise your own magickal power, too, and see how intensely you can get the energetic vibrations flowing within you. Stretch out your consciousness and see if you receive any psychic insights. Write down your impressions. Also note the intensity of the energy at its height, rating the maximum level of energy you were able to raise on a scale of 1 to 10, or if you prefer, rating it as "low," "medium," "high," or "extremely high."

Which elements yielded the best results? Did you feel comfortable with these elements, did they feel right? If so, cooperating with these forces magickally will give spellwork a powerful boost.

But what if it didn't feel right? What if your best results were with air, yet you much prefer fire? Ultimately, it's your preference that matters. These exercises that explore the elements give us clues or leads to look into, but by no means do we have to choose one element over another simply because it appears to be most effective for us. In magick, we work with all the elements, and when we select a "favorite" element to emphasize, our relationship with that element deepens, making it effective for us regardless of whether or not our natural affinities are in original agreement.

Numeric Affinities

What's your lucky number? Elements aren't the only aspects of magick for which we feel special affinities. We each have our own numeric affinities, too, and you can use this information to make your magick better.

For example, if your lucky number is 13, you probably don't want to use it in a binding tablet to stave off a foe. But if you were making a personal talisman or amulet for yourself, adding the number 13 to the object will increase its charm. Certain numbers have special connotations for us, and our specific associations for these numbers we consider "lucky" or "unlucky" are unique to each individual. Knowing your likes and your dislikes ensures your ability to use numbers in the most magickally powerful ways possible.

For instance, using your lucky number in any sort of charm or spell intended to act on you personally in a favorable manner will help the magick reach its goal. We can also use numbers to give our magick our energetic signature or personal mark when carving the number into our wand or tracing its symbol onto herbal sachets or other magickal items. If five is our lucky number, we might choose to use five stones in our spell, or tap our wand on a potion five times to give our magick an extra charge. Likewise, if we have an unlucky number, defensive and offensive spells will be strengthened if we use that number to help seal the fate of our enemies.

But what if you don't have a lucky or an unlucky number? How can you discover it? Intend to find it and you will.

Finding Numeric Affinities Exercise

Start by making a list of numbers, from one to as high as you feel like going, but at least listing through number nine. Beside each number, write a key word for the first thing that comes to mind when you think of that number, or a one-word description of the number's essence or symbolism, in your own opinion. Now circle five numbers on your list that, based on your descriptions, you seem to prefer over the others. Write these five numbers on a separate sheet of paper you will carry with you over the next few weeks. Declare your intention to discover your numeric affinities. You could say this out loud, whisper it to your best friend, write it down, or perform a dedication ritual in which you take an oath to complete your quest for a lucky number. It really doesn't matter how you state it, as long as the idea gets into the world somehow that you are seeking an answer.

Pay attention to your surroundings in the next few weeks. Does one of the numbers on your list seem to keep popping up everywhere? Is it coming up in fortunate or unfortunate circumstances? You can also experiment with writing a number on your skin, trying a new one each day and seeing if anything out of the ordinary occurs. Spellwork can give you more information, too. Try casting a short-term charm for general good luck every few days or so, each time using a different number. Which one seems to be most effective? Carry on in this manner for two to three weeks, however long feels right to you, then take another look at your list of five numbers. Is there a clear winner now? Can you scratch any numbers off the list completely? Narrow it down as much as you can based on the outcomes of your various experiments, then select your preference from what remains.

Plant Affinities

Some of us have affinities for certain plants, and featuring such plants prominently in our magick when appropriate makes spellwork more personal and effective—these botanicals will work overtime to help you. Many roads can lead you toward discovering your own plant affinities. You could explore a public garden, take a stroll in the forest, go to a gardening store, visit a flower shop, or even browse through a nature field guide, noting any plants you find especially appealing. Research each plant further and see if any species stands out. If so, try your hand at growing this plant and using it in magick. If both your gardening and your spellwork are successful, you'll know you've found the one. Even those of us who feel we have a "black thumb" can usually find a plant or two that we are able to grow successfully. Can't grow flowers? Try succulents. Can't even grow a cactus? Try moss. Through experimentation, you'll find a plant whose spirit and energy harmonizes with your own. Here's a quick questionnaire that will help narrow down a good starting point for further exploration:

Plant Affinities Questionnaire

- Would you rather stroll through a meadow of flowers and grass, walk through a forest of trees, or play around the cacti in the desert?

- Does the idea of having an affinity with a rare, exotic plant appeal to you more than the idea of having a common plant as your special friend?

- What flowers, trees, or other plants native to your area do you especially like?

- Have you ever lived in a different place, perhaps growing up in the desert and now living by a beach? If so, are there plants you miss seeing around?

- From a purely aesthetic perspective, which gift would you like best? A small cactus, a pot of flowers, a fern, or a bonsai tree?

- If someone were to give you a bouquet, what kind of flowers would you want included? If you're not sure of names, what colors or general shapes come to mind?

- What are three plants you would like to learn more about?

Take your answers, and go exploring.

Magickal Tool Affinities

Even the magickal tools we use can be chosen based on our affinities. Some people are better with wands, others with swords or staffs. Some people like brooms, while others dig bells. Whatever our sensibilities might be, using tools that work well with us and harmonize with our personal energy patterns will produce more effective magick.

You can use what you know about your other affinities to guide you in selecting the best tools. Love the moon, water, or the number three? Try a cauldron. Feel in tune with the air? Craft an air wand. Love the fire element? Stock your altar with candles. Is five your lucky number, or are you a very stable and earthy type? Try incorporating pentacles into your spellwork. Is binding magick your special skill? Put some string in your magickal tool belt and try some knotting spells.

Experimenting with tools you haven't used very often is great; doing so expands your skills and keeps things exciting, fun, and fresh. But when you're working a spell that absolutely must not fail, use a tool with which you share an affinity, a tool you know you can operate to produce the results you need.

Although your other affinities can lead you in the right direction, there's only one way to know for certain which tools are best for you personally, and that's to try them out. There is such a variety of magickal implements available, though, it would be impossible to buy or even make every one. You need somewhere to begin. Complete this survey to help narrow down the infinite possibilities:

Magickal Tool Affinities Survey
What do you need and want in a magickal tool? Rate the following characteristics in order of importance:

- Functionality—the tool efficiently fulfills its purpose
- Inherent power—the tool has inherent magickal power in the very substance it's made of or in its design
- Practicality—the tool is of a size and form that is practical for your life; in other words, you couldn't keep a full-size cauldron in a studio apartment or grow poisonous plants around curious toddlers or pets
- Ease of use
- Affordability
- Ease of construction or crafting
- Symbolism—the tool is associated with a particular deity or has particular associations such as solar or lunar, feminine or masculine, that make it especially relevant to your path
- History—the tool is a traditional tool of magick that has been used for ages and has a long and possibly documented history
- Innovation—the tool is a modern invention you feel is on the cutting edge in shaping magick's future

Once you've got your priorities rated, head to a magickal supply shop or browse the Internet and see what's available. Get ideas and inspiration for tools you might want to buy or make, keeping in mind that tools you create yourself will be more powerful. Even if you plan to purchase your tools in the long run, it makes sense to craft a homemade version first before investing in the real thing, since you won't really know if you're in tune with a tool until you try it. Sketch pictures or jot down notes, then start adding these gadgets to your tool kit one by one.

Run with It!

Now take your results from the activities in this chapter and run with them, heading to the library and to the altar for further investigation. You'll soon experience how utilizing your true affinities takes you further in your quest for better, more personalized spellcraft.

<u>EXERCISE</u>

1. What are your elemental affinities?
2. How can knowing your affinities help you craft better magick?
3. Do you believe certain numbers can be especially lucky or unlucky for particular individuals?
4. Have you ever worked a spell that emphasized and incorporated in a major way one of your personal magickal affinities? What were the results of this magick?
5. Have you ever tried to perform an act of magick with ingredients or tools you hate? What were the results?

Taking It Further

Magick is largely a matter of taste. So what's yours? Do you notice any patterns or particular styles or interests emerging as you explore your affinities for tools, plants, and more? Do you seem to favor light and airy happy things, transformative and flashy mysterious things, substantial and solid reliable things, dark and indifferent destructive things? Look at all your magickal affinities, the ones you already knew and those just discovered, and see if you can find anything in common between them. If you can step back and objectively evaluate your affinities and preferences, you'll have a signpost to guide you toward further developing and refining your own unique witching style.

6

Spiritual Development

No one can be "on" all the time. Sometimes we feel so full of spirit and so close to the powers that be; other times, we might as well be a million miles away from anything even remotely sacred, feeling hollow and isolated. Our spiritual development has its ups and downs, and what triggers these fluctuations is unique to each of us. When we feel spiritually empty, we have no motivation for our magick, our intent is only halfhearted, and our spells fall flat. On the other hand, when we're enjoying a vibrant spiritual life, we shine with magickal power and our spells work miracles.

Our spirituality is directly linked to our intent, setting the tone and the limits for our magick. Intent can be summed up as "what's in your heart," the true nature of your desires and beliefs. These desires and beliefs manifest as our magickal goals, reflecting what the spirit hopes to achieve, and magick is only as good as the intent behind it.

Keeping our spiritual life fresh and thriving enables us to use magickal intent more fully and precisely. Contemplating spiritual matters and trying out new ways to connect to the greater universe makes our goals and the extent of our power much clearer. Once we know where we're at spiritually, we can put our magick in full alignment, reaching greater goals and producing outstanding results. Let's begin.

Paradoxes to Ponder

Light and dark, joy and sorrow, life and death—the world is founded on duality! This duality often manifests in the form of paradox, and within these great paradoxes of existence spiritual truths may be found. Ponder the following:

Togetherness and Separation

The ultimate goal of many spiritual systems is oneness with deity, union with the sacred source of all. We might imagine escaping our bodies and merging completely with God and Goddess, our consciousness fully absorbed into the consciousness of godhead.

The moment we entirely unite, however, we cease to exist as separate entities. We become the things we merge into, and therefore there is no togetherness, no separate perception with which to experience that with which we've joined. We *must* be separate entities, individuals apart from each other, in order to perceive and enjoy togetherness. I must be me in order to see you; if we are one, there is no "us."

Imagine a strand of holiday lights, and imagine a current of electricity as deity, the sacred energy and origin of all. We can't see a flow of electricity. Only when that electricity flows through the electric cord, into each separate colored glass bulb, do we see the electricity as red, blue, green, gold. Every person is like one of these little lights, each with our own hue and brightness. Our spirits are poured into these separate bodily (and ethereal) containers so that we can perceive and connect with each other, so that we can see the different parts of the all before we become one with it.

Perhaps the experience of life on earth allows us to retain our separate quality even when we are merged together and one with deity, so that as the macrocosm, we can remain aware of the infinite qualities and myriad of characteristics of the microcosm that lies within it. We are separate here so that we may be together there, so that when all is one, we can still recognize the little parts of that one that might have formerly been known as "Grandma," "dear old Spot," or "friendship." Our separation from deity is the very thing required for communion with deity. When we're one, we're one, unless we've first learned how to be more.

Creation and Destruction

Birth inevitably leads to death. Death inevitably leads to birth. The lion eats the gazelle, and the destruction of the gazelle creates new body mass in the lion. Our bodies die and decay, and the soil is nurtured, sustaining fresh vegetation. With the winter comes the spring, and if it weren't for the desolation and destruction of the coldest season, new growth would not emerge. Summer would be perpetual and the creation of new life would be stagnant. In order to have fresh emergence, new creation and life, we must have the ebbing, destruction, and death that come with it.

Within and Without You

We hear it said in witchy circles quite often: "If you can't find the God and Goddess within you, you won't find them anywhere." True, in a sense, but the expression is often misinterpreted and taken to mean that every individual is automatically godly, as divine and complete as any entity who has ever been called into the circle. Aren't we missing something? A bucket of sand is not the beach. If we are indeed equal to the gods, why bother honoring "outside" deities or asking for their aid? The divine essence within us exists as our own inner zero point field of infinite potentials. If it is not realized and actualized, the god within you might as well be a lump of coal. It takes an understanding and awareness of the broader divine essence that exists outside of your being, encompassing not only you but everything else in existence, too, in order to find this same essence within yourself. We must connect and align the divine essence within us to the divine essence without us in order to activate and live up to our divine potential. Truly, if we can't find the God and Goddess within, we won't find them without, but it is equally true that if we can't find the God and Goddess without, we won't find them within.

Questioning Is Essential!

In addition to pondering these and other great mysteries of existence, questioning is essential in your spiritual development. Below are some questions to help you map out your own route to spiritual progress. Focus on one or two questions at a time, contemplating the matter and writing down your thoughts until you feel you have the answer or you're drawn to move on to a different question. You may want to spend several days or even weeks contemplating the questions you find most interesting.

Many of these questions are unanswerable in that they don't lend themselves to clear and definitive solutions. Still, the journey you take to reach your conclusions will open up new levels of awareness and knowledge to enlighten your spirit and empower your magick.

- If humanity were to progress in a positive direction, what would it look like? What would cease to exist, and what would come into being?

- If you had greater magickal power, what would you be able to do?

- What is the limit of your consciousness? What can you imagine lies beyond that perceived boundary?

- Is there such a thing as sheer joy or sheer sorrow, or are these two sides of the same coin?

- If you were to "become one with Goddess and God," or merge back into the origin of all, meshing fully with the sacred, would you still be you?

- What has hurt you the most in this life? Does that experience shape your present thoughts, emotions, magick, and actions?
- What would happen if you stopped owning your painful memories?
- What would happen if you let go of hate, anger, guilt?
- If your biggest dreams come true, what will that look like and what will you do differently? How will your perceptions and attitudes change?
- What would it feel like to be a plant? A non-human animal? An alien from another world? A different person on this planet, wealthy, poor, a person in the midst of war?
- If you were to be inducted into a council of spiritual leaders including Buddha, Jesus, Mohammed, Meher Baba, the Dalai Lama, and others, what would you personally bring to the table? What could you teach this group? What would be your special niche?
- What do you know that no one else knows?

Exercises for Spiritual Development

Trying out different activities to further your spiritual development keeps you excited to see what comes next. With each step forward you take, your magick will grow deeper and more meaningful in reflection. Here are some exercises you might find helpful in shaking up your spiritual routine.

Making Out with the Elements

This exercise offers a unique way to experience the elements in a brand new light and hopefully gain further spiritual understanding along the way. Fix yourself up like you would if you were preparing for an exciting night of romance with someone fabulous. Wear something that makes you feel attractive, preferably something made of a thin, breathable fabric. If you have a safe and private area in which you can do so, you might want to skip clothing altogether. Just be sure to put safety first. Once you're ready, go outside with a candle and a bowl of water. Light the candle, and lay on the ground beside it, gazing lustily at the flame. See its beauty; feel its power and its changeable nature. Do you notice any qualities of the fire element you've never paid attention to before? Next pick up a handful of dirt and rub it on your skin, caressing yourself and enjoying the feel of the cool earth. Are you aware of any essences of the earth element you've never before sensed? Now dip your fingers into the bowl of water and slowly trace patterns on your skin, feeling the wetness as the water element seeps into your body. Are you getting any new impressions about the water element? The wind is next; stretch your arms and legs open wide and feel the air all over you. How does it feel? Do you sense any unfamiliar energies in the air element? Lay quietly for awhile and just feel, enjoying the earth and the sensations it brings to your body and soul. When you're finished, record your thoughts with music, art, or dance.

Painting the All

This exercise lets your spirit take the reins. Get some inexpensive paints and a canvas or a piece of scrap wood or paper. Set out your supplies and state your intention to paint absolutely whatever comes through you. If it suits your fancy, invite a specific deity or spirit to use you as a medium. Then quiet your mind, doing your best to think nothing. Start painting freely, not thinking and not looking, letting sensation guide you. Once you're done, stand back and gaze at your picture. Do you see any images or words in the paint strokes? What feelings or thoughts does the painting invoke? Relax with a cup of tea or hot chocolate and enjoy your art.

Loving the Haters

Compassion is a beautiful thing, and when we can love the ones who hate, it's a sign of true spiritual evolution. Practicing feeling compassion for your enemies and those you dislike opens your heart and spirit to new insights and energies.

Focus your thoughts on someone you absolutely despise; see them in your mind in all their hideous glory. It need not be someone you know personally, for instance, you could choose an oppressive dictator or a local violent thug. Now picture the person reversing in age, going from adult to teen to child to tiny helpless infant. See yourself holding that baby in your arms; gaze at it lovingly. Imagine laying the infant to rest in a crib, carefully covering it with a warm blanket. End the visualization with a loving feeling in your heart, take a deep breath, and exhale deeply, knowing that you have made progress in your spiritual development into a more compassionate being.

Seeking and Finding

This spiritual development exercise encourages you to delve deeper and actively seek out answers in your quest for greater power and enlightenment. Choose a selection of reference materials, sources that have special meaning for you or that you feel contain spiritual truth. Your selection might include a tarot deck or two, several sacred texts from various traditions, your own Book of Shadows, a book of nature poetry or artistic masterpieces—whatever you feel might be a beneficial reference in your quest for spiritual answers.

Place the references around you. On a piece of paper, write down one of your biggest questions about magick, spirituality, or existence. Close your eyes. One by one, consult your reference materials, randomly opening each book and letting your finger land on a passage, or mixing your tarot deck and choosing a card or cards. Think about each message. Does it give you any insight into your question? Write down any new thoughts and impressions. Place your notes in your purse or pocket and carry them with you for a few days. Think of your question each night before going to sleep and each morning upon waking. After several days, read over your notes and reevaluate your question. Are you closer to an answer? Repeat the exercise until you are.

Help Is on the Way!

Ever feel kind of lonely in your spiritual quest? We all do sometimes, but luckily help is never far away. When you're feeling spiritually isolated or in need of assistance, it might be time to have a nice long talk with your spirit guides. Spirit guides are disembodied souls that act as guides and assistants, offering us help with our magick and inspiring our spiritual development. Spirit guides are our magickal BFFs, and although we might forget about them from time to time, it's well worth the trouble to stay in touch.

It's comforting to remember that although we are ultimately responsible for our own spiritual development, even solitary practitioners don't have to go it alone. Whether you're a member of a coven or you practice your craft alone in your bedroom late at night, each of us has our own personal spiritual assistant, possibly even a team of assistants.

Chances are, you've made their acquaintance in one way or another. You might know your guides very well, inside and out, or perhaps you've worked with them a good bit but have so far caught only glimpses of their appearance. Maybe you know some of your guides, but could there be others you haven't met yet? However well acquainted, wouldn't you like to find out more about them? Maybe you've never sensed your spirit guide, but you're curious to investigate further. As we become more aware of them, they become exceedingly helpful in all types of magickal and spiritual work.

Spirit guides can help you communicate with the dead, connect with deity, and summon the elements. They can assist you in all manner of spellwork and lead you toward deeper spirituality and greater magickal power.

Whether you already know your guides but want to know them better, or you're looking to meet your guides for the very first time, the following techniques will expand your awareness of these beings and fortify your friendship. Try this:

Over Your Shoulder

This exercise encourages you to discover more about your spirit guides through pure sensation and psychic awareness. Go into a dark room or safe outdoor area totally alone. Close your eyes and tune in to the energy field around you. Do you sense anyone else present? What do you feel? Mentally call on your guides and ask that they reveal themselves to you. Are you getting any impressions or feelings?

Notice as much detail as you can. If you like, ask questions of your guides. When you're done, if you were able to sense your spirit guides, write down everything you remember about the experience, or draw an image of your impressions. If your attempt is not successful, repeat the exercise every day until you get positive results.

Face Cards

This exercise uses the tarot to uncover hidden characteristics of your spirit guides. Focus on one of the guides you would like to know more about. Politely ask the guide to reveal its identity. Mix your tarot deck and draw any cards that seem to call to you. When you're finished, thank your guide, then write down your interpretation of the cards you drew in relation to how they might describe your guide.

Be a Pal

Building up strong relationships with your guides takes effort, but it doesn't have to take a lot of time. Give your guides thanks every day, share your fears and dreams with them, and show genuine interest in who they truly are as spirits. Set out small gifts and offerings for your guides, or play some special music just for them. Be friendly and good to your guides, and your guides will be good to you.

Spirit Communication

If you've ever communicated with spirits of the dead, you know how the practice can benefit your spiritual development, expanding beliefs of what is possible and allowing a broader perspective on the mysteries of existence. Using spirit communication techniques to connect with souls who have "left the building" increases awareness and can also potentially soothe old wounds left from unresolved matters between the living and the dead.

If you've never communicated with late friends and relatives or if it's been a while since you've done so, you might want to give it a go using a more personalized approach. Consider your affinities and adapt spirit communication methods to take full advantage of your unique energies. For instance, if you feel drawn to rivers and oceans, wetting your hands and your face will aid you in making contact with the dead. Likewise, if you feel in tune with the element fire, you'll benefit from incorporating candles in your spirit communication rituals. If you have a close bond with earth, try smearing dirt on your face before you begin. If air is your favorite, try stirring up the spirits by waving a handheld fan. When we utilize our affinities, we express our truest essence and create a vibration of trust and magick between ourselves and the spirits we want to contact.

Those who have had past experiences with ghosts can look to these incidents for clues to finding their own most effective methods. Were you standing, sitting, or lying down when you had your most profound experiences? Were you outside or inside? Were you hungry or full? Were you alone or with friends? Were your eyes closed or open? Mimicking the conditions of previous ghostly encounters helps create an environment conducive to spirit communication.

There are many ways to interact with spirits of the dead, and your particular motives for doing so will guide you toward an appropriate method. If you need to obtain detailed information from the spirit, for instance, a talking board or automatic writing is an ideal option. For a more casual and abstract conversation, try talking through spirit art, runes, or the tarot. When simple yes or no answers from the spirit will do, leaves, incense smoke, water, wind, stones, or flame will be effective tools. If your desire is to commune with the spirit in a shared experience, dancing, spirit-guided walking, singing, or meditation will serve you well. If you suspect you are gifted when it comes to spirit communication, try your hand at direct mediumship, allowing yourself to be a channel through which the dead may speak.

Research various forms of spirit communication that are new to you, then try in turn all the techniques you feel comfortable using. You'll soon discover the forms of spirit communication you're best at. Of course, it's still a good idea to switch it up now and then. Interacting with the dead in many ways offers us the experience and excitement we need to discover and remember layers of spirituality that would otherwise be unknown or forgotten.

That's the Spirit!

By intending to spiritually progress, we do. Trying new things, contemplating, questioning, meditating, and seeking ways to connect to spirits other than our own propel us forward in our spiritual development. Achieving greater spirituality is a personal and intimate quest. See into the distance, map your route, and get there.

EXERCISE

Spirituality means something different to everyone. Answer these questions to help define for yourself what you truly seek.

1. What is your vision of enlightenment? Picture yourself as a spiritually evolved being and note the details and characteristics of the image.
2. Do you believe in any higher powers or deities? Why or why not? If you do, think about each one and do your best to describe its nature and essence. If not, do your best to describe your own soul in what you imagine would be its most harmonic state.
3. Have you witnessed any evidence of spirit existing beyond the physical form? Do you believe that it does? Why or why not? How would it change your life if you believed the opposite of what you believe now?
4. What are your biggest spiritual questions? Name at least three and write down what you will do to seek out the answers.

Taking It Further

Keeping our spiritual waters flowing takes making some waves every now and then. Pushing yourself into unfamiliar spiritual territory is one way to further your development and inspire new ideas. Honestly, is there a branch of Paganism or other religious discipline you find a little on the stupid or revolting side? Is there a branch of Paganism or other religious discipline that intrigues you? Read a little about one of each, something you like and something you dislike. Then write about why you agree or disagree. Questioning and reaching into the world of spirit through a multitude of methods are the keys to spiritual development and the foundation of informed magickal intent.

7

Psychic Spellwork

Most likely, you're no stranger to psychic insight, and you probably already have a firm idea of what extra-sensory perception
(ESP) means. But don't let that prior experience become a limit, fenc-
ing you into the confines of familiarity and restricting your psychic
potential to what you already know is possible. When we think of psychic awareness, the first thing that comes to mind might be premoni-
tions, those quick flashes of insight that "give us a feeling" that can
be neither explained nor denied. But psychic awareness encompasses
much more than this. It is not only the ability to perceive reality outside of its usual confines; it is the ability to see the energetic structure
of the whole, the parts, and the connections between them. It is the
vision to find the key to the mystery amidst all the clutter.

Let's make further use of our holiday lights analogy from the previous chapter to illustrate another way to look at psychic awareness. Like the universe, the string of lights is comprised solely of energy. The cord, the bulbs, the flowing current, the filament, the light emitted—all are essentially energy. Each bulb is analogous to each of our bodies; just as each bulb acts as a container for the light, each human body acts as a container for spirit, imparting its own hue as the energy flows through it. Now imagine consciousness focused within each tiny bulb. That consciousness might think, "I'm a green light" or "I'm red." This limited light bulb consciousness is akin to our everyday awareness, our non-psychic mind. Now, if that tiny bulb had a psychic sense, it would not only be aware of itself as a red light or a green light, but it would also be conscious of the cord, the other bulbs, the current running throughout the whole contraption. Not only that, it would be aware of the string of lights as a whole; it would be aware of the multitude of components both as a collective whole and as distinct units. This expanded light bulb consciousness is analogous with our psychic awareness, perceiving both the parts and the whole simultaneously. Psychic awareness gives us a direct view into the fabric of the universe, into the threads we unravel and re-weave in magick. It is in fact a skill inextricably linked with magick, and without it, spells are doomed.

Attempting magick without ESP is like a mechanic trying to fix a car without any tools: it just doesn't work. If we can't sense energies, we can't code those energies, and it is the coding of energy that makes magick happen. Psychic awareness, spirituality, and magick are in fact triple aspects of a single process, the way in which we relate to the divine energies that course throughout the whole of creation. Psychic awareness is the perception of these energies, spirituality is communion with these energies, and magick is the manipulation, or coding, of these energies. ESP is magickal consciousness itself; it allows us to perceive and understand the energies needed to make spells succeed.

But ESP not only makes magick possible, it can also be utilized through a variety of techniques to make magick more powerful and effective. Once you discover the greater potential of psychic awareness, connecting to the energies in natural magickal ingredients is easier. You're able to foresee problems in your life before they arise. Through proactive spellwork, you'll be able to nip hardships in the bud. You have a means for discerning potential obstacles and stumbling blocks that would otherwise hinder magickal success, giving you the information needed to build into the initial design of your spell solutions to overcome these challenges. Your skill at working magick spanning long distances improves, and you're better able to pinpoint exactly where on earth your magickal power is most needed. Right now, let's take a deeper look at the many ways ESP can be implemented to make magick more effective.

ESP for Easier Natural Magick

Knowing the traditional attributes of an herb is one thing. Psychically sensing firsthand the consciousness and vibrations of the particular bit of plant you hold in your palm right now is quite another. ESP provides a way to perceive energies in natural objects, and the closer we look, the more magickal power and potential we see.

Before empowering the herbs, stones, and other ingredients you might use in a ritual, take time to fully connect with the energies residing within each substance. Notice not only what you're looking for, but see also the entirety of energies present. For example, say you have an apple you're using in a love charm. You're aware of the romance-inducing attributes of apples, and if that is the only energetic quality you expect to find in the apple, then find it you will, but you're not likely to notice much more. If instead you approach the fruit with a clear mind, open to receiving any and all impressions, you'll sense much more than just the love energy in the apple. You'll see as well the particular qualities of that particular apple, sense its journey from tree to market, and intuit the specific information and vibes stored within the fruit's unique flesh, seeds, and core.

Hold the herb or stone in your hands. Clear your head of thoughts related to the spell you're planning. Open your senses to the object, approaching it in the same way you might perform psychometry on a piece of jewelry or other personal item. Try to sense the object's history and its present energetic state. What transformations has it undergone? What energetic processes are occurring within it right now? Refrain from projecting your own thoughts and imaginings, but be open to any impressions that come to you.

Are you receiving any images or sensations that could be used to help your spell succeed? By connecting with natural magickal ingredients in this less expectant, more psychometric, manner (as opposed to proceeding straightaway to tuning in to the particular attributes relevant to the spellwork at hand), you invite the possibility of gaining knowledge that can be used to make your magick work better.

For example, you might psychically discover that the tree that grew the nutmeg you bought to use in a healing sachet underwent and overcame a serious botanical illness last winter. Knowing more about the plant's power and abilities, you would then be better able to draw on the nutmeg's unique energies and its prior experience of tenacity and successful recovery when you empower the herb for use in your healing charm. Asking a little more of your psychic sense lends your natural magick more ease and effectiveness.

ESP Keeps Trouble at Bay

We've all heard of preventive medicine—how about preventive magick? Too often, we turn to spellwork only after trouble has arisen, after the problem has escalated to a level of wreaking pure havoc. With ESP, we have the potential to sense trouble looming on the horizon, and we can often knock it back with spellwork to keep the problem from ever manifesting itself in our reality.

We sometimes get a feeling that "something isn't right"; we feel anxious or worried for no apparent reason. As ESP develops, these hunches become more detailed. We come to sense major changes milling at the workplace, we know intuitively when a relative is nearing danger, we know ahead of time when a slanderous tongue is about to do its worst. Psychic foresight shows us what is likely to happen if we don't act, and through this information, we *can* act, using magick more effectively as a preventive measure to help stop trouble before it strikes.

Periodically, take a few moments to sit back and sense the general energetic atmosphere surrounding you. Focus your thoughts outside of yourself and into nothing in particular. What do you sense approaching? What do you sense moving away? Are any forces present that intend to protect or harm you? Through psychic awareness, you can take stock of potential trouble and magickally combat the situation through proactive spellwork. For instance, if you were to psychically perceive an approaching economic hardship, you could lessen the burden through preventive wealth-bringing magick, frugality, and resourcefulness ahead of time, before you find yourself knee deep in the poor swamp.

ESP helps us put our magickal abilities to timely, practical use. With ESP, we don't have to wait around for trouble to descend upon us. We can sense trouble before it arrives and often stave it off successfully through the power of preventive magick.

ESP Gets Spells Over Humps

Sometimes our spells fail due to unforeseen obstacles. Say we cast a spell to bring creative inspiration to help us finish up an important project. Such a spell might do just that, but if an unexpected illness or other obligations arise, that magickal inspiration will likely go to waste. With ESP, you can check for potential obstacles such as these before you ever wave a wand, and you can tweak your spells to overcome these challenges from the get go so that magick will work.

For example, suppose you're about to craft an herbal charm to manifest a move to a different city, and through psychic awareness, you determine there might be financial obstacles. You could use that information to remove the potential impediment to your magick, adding a wealth-bringing herb such as cinnamon or patchouli to the charm and clearing the way for your spell's success.

When you need to work magick, help ensure its success by using your ESP to illuminate any challenges or obstacles your spell might face. Sit quietly and pose to your psychic mind the question, "What obstacles might hinder my spell?" Clear your mind and note new thoughts as they spring forth into being.

Another way to employ ESP to check for spell obstacles is through a divination method such as tarot. For example, before you design a spell, you could ask yourself, "What could possibly thwart this magick?" Then you could draw a few tarot cards, cast the runes, or use another divination technique, interpreting indications to ascertain potential obstacles that threaten to trip up your spell.

Whether gained through divination or direct awareness, use your psychically obtained knowledge to help ensure magickal success. Craft solutions to possible problems into your spell design, making changes and adding extras in order to give your magick the best chance for success. Could poor health be an obstacle? Add a purification bath to your ritual. Does a calamity threaten to throw a wrench in your magickal plans to obtain a lover? Perform a protective charm along with your love spell and counteract the danger. ESP acts as a scout for magick, running ahead and spotting potential roadblocks so we can choose the very best path for our spells and give our magick the backup it needs to succeed.

Close-Up Magick at a Distance

ESP also makes it easier to perform magick at a distance, enabling powerful spellwork from any location aimed at any place on the planet. Performing a spell to affect the energies in your own backyard is considerably easier than working a spell to affect a change at a town thousands of miles away. With psychic awareness, however, we can tune in to any locale and direct our magick to manipulate energies both near and far.

When you're working magick aimed at a far away target, you'll get better results if you go beyond simply imagining and visualizing the place where your spell is headed. Remote viewing lets your psychic sense actually go to the location and work the spell there through your spiritual body. Focus your thoughts on the place; direct your spiritual body to travel there. See the location in the now, not from imagination, but through psychic sensation. Notice the details and be receptive to any emotions and ideas you might pick up on. What do you see? What do you feel? What information are you receiving?

Another method for psychically connecting at a distance involves the magick circle. Cast the circle in the usual manner, sending energy out through your wand, hand, or ritual blade to form a protective sphere around your workspace. Don't close the circle completely. Instead, stop just short of the 360-degree mark, leaving the stream of energy between the circle and the tool you're using connected and intact. Now, direct your attention to a map or globe that has been previously placed in your ritual area. Continue wrapping the circle around the location where your spell is focused, casting it psychically as you symbolically trace its outline around the place name on the globe or map. This double magick circle creates a psychic connection that allows you to be in two places at once. You're in your actual physical location carrying out the physical aspects of the spell, and you're also at the place to where the spell is directed, carrying out the psychic, mental, and spiritual aspects of the spell.

Whether you get there through creative circle casting or through the straightforward exercise of direct psychic awareness, once you've tuned in to the target location, proceed with the spell as if you are working it from the place where you intend to send it. Be there in mind and spirit as you carry out each step of the ritual process, raising energy, coding it, and releasing it up close, right where it is needed.

ESP for More Effective Magickal Activism

ESP can also be used to increase the efficiency and effectiveness of magickal activism, allowing us to pinpoint exactly where on earth our spell efforts are most needed. We have magickal abilities for a reason, that reason being to help make things better for ourselves, for each other, our planet, and all life that inhabits it. Lending our magickal power to help relieve the suffering of whoever or whatever we care about is a responsibility we all bear. We must do what we can on every level, addressing problems and finding solutions from multiple angles. With psychic awareness, such magickal efforts can be better focused, and spells can be directed more precisely to wherever they will have the most positive and powerful effect.

For example, suppose you're passionate about animal welfare, and you're especially interested in helping abused dogs. You could take some time each day to do a general spell for the protection of all dogs, or you could use your ESP to scan the earth, honing in on individual dogs currently being abused, and focusing your spellwork to send immediate protection directly to those particular dogs.

Our magick might not yet be powerful enough to save the world, but it's certainly strong enough to save some aspect of the world, especially when concentrated through specific spells targeted to affect specific situations. If you're interested in trying some magickal activism, think of who or what you want to help, sit back and relax, and psychically search the world, extending your awareness to perceive current events relevant to your cause. Focus in on a vivid impression, sensing as many details as possible. Then craft a spell to positively change the situation, based on what needs to be done and on what you intuit to be your best angle for doing so.

For example, suppose your psychic awareness hones in on a particular logging company about to destroy a particular tract of forest, and you decide you want to use your magick to help stop the destruction. Through ESP, you know exactly where to send your spell, and you have a specific target. You could then choose from what side you want to approach the problem. For instance, in this example, you could decide to do a spell to bind the logging machinery, causing it to stop working. Or you could shield the forest with protective energies. Or you could summon spirits or deities you believe to be guardians of the trees, calling them into defensive action. There are unlimited ways in which you could use magick to positively affect the situation, and your psychic awareness can both inspire and harness your creativity in spell design. However you approach it, using ESP to help better concentrate power where it's needed most maximizes the benefits, impact, and effectiveness of magickal activism.

Psychism vs. Paranoia: Fact-Checking ESP

Of course, it's a fine line between psychism and paranoia. With putting trust in psychic power comes the risk of mistaking suspicions and paranoia for true intuitive hunches, and it's sometimes difficult to separate imagination from ESP. While it's wise to trust your intuition to a certain extent, it's wiser still to check the accuracy of the psychic impressions you receive.

You can fact-check your ESP by making phone calls, checking the news, etc.; don't jump to conclusions before you check it out through mundane means!

Psychic Success

Now that you know the benefits and applications of psychic awareness in magick, you can use these skills to increase the power and effectiveness of your spells. Psychic spellwork puts a new twist on familiar modes of magick, relighting the spark of mystical discovery, and bringing your skills and talents to the fore. By using your psychic abilities to their full magickal capacity, you can make your spellcasting more successful, strong, precise, and progressive.

EXERCISE

How might you use ESP to help the following acts of magick succeed? Think of at least two ways ESP could benefit each spell.

1. A spell to protect threatened rivers
2. An herbal tea to banish sorrow
3. A spell to land a promotion
4. A spell to heal a sick friend in a foreign country
5. A spell to ward off general misfortune

Taking It Further

In what other ways can psychic power make magick more effective? Is more advanced, lofty spellwork in reach now that you understand how

ESP can help maximize magickal results? Study ways to increase psychic awareness, practice divination, and brainstorm new applications for utilizing ESP for better magick. Psychic spellwork is far more powerful than spells wrought without intuition, and mastering these skills will bring new potency and accuracy to your magick.

8

Psychic Development

As related to magickal consciousness, we know psychic awareness is a skill intrinsic to spellwork, but without active development, our psychic sense can get a little rusty. Psychic awareness has three aspects: perceiving the whole, the parts, and the connections between them. Exploring these aspects in new ways gives you the tools and the edge you need to shake the dust off your psychic sense and give your ESP a well-rounded education. The more psychic you become, the better and more effective your magick is. Developing psychic skills is not difficult or time-consuming; in fact, exercising your ESP is a simple and convenient way to sneak fun and mystical mini-breaks into your day. Whether you can spare half an hour or just a few minutes, every time you practice developing your ESP, you'll benefit. Let's take a look at some unusual but effective methods for developing these skills.

ESP's Three Aspects

You've heard the expression of someone being unable to "see the forest for the trees." Well, ESP is like seeing not only the forest and the trees, but also the living energy of the air, earth, and root systems that run between them. Taking another example, if you were fully using your psychic sense to gain awareness of the crowd at a football game, you would perceive each fan individually (the parts), the crowd as a united entity (the whole), and the stadium itself (the connections between them). Sounds tricky, but it's really pretty easy if you break it down and focus on each distinct aspect. Let's take a look at what ESP's three aspects really are, and explore some practical and effective ways for developing each skill.

Perceiving the Whole

This aspect of ESP allows you to see the "big picture." Perceiving the whole means being aware of the all-inclusive underlying patterns and overriding themes that permeate reality. Perceiving the whole might be psychically experienced as a general feeling that can't be pinned to one specific individual, such as a hunch about shifts in society or major transformations of the planet. Magickally speaking, perceiving the whole equates to the spellcaster being aware of the overall energy involved in a particular magick working. When you're performing magick, take a moment to be aware of all the energy present. Don't focus only on the herbs in front of you or only on the goddess energy you just summoned. See it all together: get a feel for the magick and all energies involved as a whole, as one single feeling, thought, or emotion.

Exercise to Perceive the Whole

Try this exercise to help you develop this first aspect of ESP. Stand outside quietly, silencing your mental chatter and mundane worries.

Empty your mind as much as possible. Try to avoid thinking about anything or anyone in particular. Once you're in this state, turn your consciousness back on and radiate it outward to span across the entire planet, going all the way up to the stars if you like, perhaps stretching your awareness even further to perceive distant galaxies. What do you sense? You will most likely experience this type of psychic awareness as a feeling or pure emotion you can then interpret to gain a picture of the overall state of affairs for mankind. Keep a journal of your experiences and perceptions, and check the news regularly to see if it bears evidence in support of your psychic sensations.

Perceiving the Parts

This aspect of ESP is like seeing those individual trees that make up the metaphorical forest. Perceiving the parts means being aware of separate and distinct energies as separate and distinct energies. This aspect of psychic perception is often experienced as a feeling, emotion, or an image relating to a specific person, place, or thing. For example, if you were to get a vision of a faraway cousin burning her hand on the stove, you would be psychically perceiving the parts, seeing the individual part of reality called your cousin.

In magick, perceiving the parts relates to the steps of magick in which we sense the distinct energies of each spell component. Consciously honing in on and perceiving the healing energies in lavender, so that the specific vibration of healing can be drawn to the surface and amplified through an empowering rite is one example. Take a moment to notice each distinct energy you are using in your magick. If you're planning on using sage in a divination blend, for instance, notice the other energies in the herb, each nuance and every unique vibration, before focusing in on the specific energy you're looking for.

EXERCISE TO PERCEIVE THE PARTS

Here's an exercise to develop your skill in psychically perceiving the parts, your ability to be aware of distinct, specific energies as individual units. Choose an herb with multiple magickal attributes. For this example, we'll use cinnamon, but any herb (or stone) with more than one energetic property will do fine.

Hold the cinnamon in your hand. Now see if you can direct your ESP to sense the vibration in cinnamon that makes it a good ingredient for a passion-inducing spell. Do you sense an exciting energy, the vibration of physical passion? Write down what you perceive. Next, after taking a moment to clear your head, see if you can focus in on cinnamon's wealth-bringing attribute. Do you sense a richness, an energy of multiplication or manifestation, the vibration of prosperity and plenty? Make a note of your impressions. Now, after once more preparing your mind for a fresh try, hold the cinnamon and this time concentrate on perceiving within the cinnamon the very energy you are using to perceive it, the attribute of cinnamon that makes it an excellent choice for ESP-boosting blends. Do you feel an opening or vibration within the cinnamon that acts as a gateway to pure magickal power? Write down what you sense. Now look at your results. Were you successful? Could you sense some parts, but not others? Keep trying, adding another attribute to your psychic search each time you repeat the exercise.

Perceiving the Connections

This third and final aspect of ESP is probably the trickiest, but it's also the aspect that provides the very foundation of magickal action. Perceiving the connections means being aware of the magickal power coursing throughout the creation, separating and grouping energies and holding these energies together in distinct forms. Perceiving the connections between the parts and the whole of reality is like seeing the glue that binds it all together, the magickal power that surrounds and connects each part of the all to the all itself.

This psychic skill lets us see the mirror responsible for producing the reflections we know as "real life." Perceiving the connections is often experienced as a sensation of timelessness or "place-lessness," an awareness of a continuum or thread of energy running between distinct parts. For example, when a person experiences déjà vu, they are perceiving the connections that run between the past and the present.

The present location or circumstance in the present time is connected to the past location or circumstance in the past time in which the same sensations were previously experienced, and our psychic ability to perceive this connection results in the sensation we call déjà vu.

Magickally, this aspect of ESP is the road on which spells travel. We sense the connections between the moon and the goddess, between the symbol on our altar and all the symbol represents. When working magick, don't focus solely on the vehicle (spell ingredients, tools, etc.) or on the destination (the spell's ultimate goal). Take a look at the road you use to get that energy where it needs to go, psychically perceiving the connections between the parts and the whole of the magick.

EXERCISE TO PERCEIVE THE CONNECTIONS

This exercise will strengthen your ability to psychically perceive connections between energies. Select three rocks, two of the same type and one with a distinctly different energy pattern. Two quartz crystals and one hematite stone make a good combination. Place the rocks on a table in front of you and hold your hand above the stones, moving it over all the stones and then over each stone individually. Notice how close your hand needs to be to the stones in order for you to sense their energies, and try to see how far away you can be and still pick up the vibes.

Now pick up two of the stones, the odd one out and one of the other two stones. Take one in each hand, sensing the energies of each. Now slowly move the stones toward each other, not to the point where they touch, but about six inches or so apart. Can you psychically sense the energy running between them? If so, see if you can move the stones further apart and still sense the connecting energy. If not, move the stones closer until you sense it. What qualities does this energy have? Write down your impressions.

Now repeat this process using the two stones of the same type. Is it easier to sense the connection with the stones that are similar to each other? What qualities does this energy have? Are you able to hold these stones farther apart than you were able to do with the two different stones and still feel the connecting energy? Note your results, and keep practicing to improve your ability to sense the energies and connections from greater and greater physical distances.

Three Sides of the Same Coin

The three aspects of ESP—perceiving the whole, the parts, and the connections between them—are in fact all integral components of our psychic sense. You can't really have one without the others. By working to develop each distinct aspect of ESP, you are strengthening each part that comprises the whole of your psychic sense, and you gain greater awareness of how these parts and wholes are all connected through your consciousness to pure magickal power.

ESP is a basic skill every witch should master. If you already have, great, keep it going and keep developing it even further so it won't fade. And if you haven't yet focused on developing your ESP, do it. You'll be amazed at how much your magick (and your spirit) will benefit.

EXERCISE

1. What are the three aspects of ESP? Can you think of other aspects of psychic awareness not covered here?
2. Which aspect of ESP are you currently best at?
3. Which aspect of ESP do you most want to develop?
4. How does ESP play a role in magick?
5. Why is it important to you personally to develop your psychic skills?

Taking It Further

The psychic mind is the magickal mind, the whole mind. When our psychic abilities are highly developed, they never turn off. We see our consciousness as a whole entity, not separated or divided into levels and layers of perceptions. We recognize that the parts, the whole, and the connections between them are all essentially one thing: magickal power. Do you think this is true? Why or why not? Contemplate the possibility of magick without ESP. Do you think it's possible? If so, how would it be done?

Strengthen your psychic sense regularly, through daily practice and by seeking out new ways to build these skills. Exploring divination techniques, studying self-hypnosis methods, and meditation will all further your psychic development, and your magickal abilities will skyrocket.

9

Divination: Secrets and Strategies
for Success

Underlying the everyday happenings in our lives are energetic forces, and through divination, the patterns and cycles of these forces can be perceived, enabling us to understand the root cause and pure essence of our experiences. Divination provides us not only a means for seeing into the past, present, and future, but it can also be used for guidance in setting life, spiritual, and magickal goals.

Whether you're using a crystal ball, tea leaves, or tarot cards, the purpose of these tools is the same: to put the seer into a psychic trance where the intricacies of energies can be both perceived and communicated. Some need no tools at all.

As our intuitive flashes and psychic visions can sometimes be misinterpreted, it's important to get an overview of the whole picture before discussing specifics. Likewise, choose words wisely when revealing any negative predictions. A good fortune-teller has the skill to communicate to the inquirer what is necessary to do in order to create a more positive future.

Divination is truly a magickal art, involving skill, creativity, practice, patience, and expression. However, with these and divination tips and tricks the pros use, you'll find your success as a seer instantly increase.

Psychic Drain Solutions

If you're experienced in the art of divination, you know exactly how draining it can be. Usually we're fine doing a reading or two, but when we get ourselves into situations where we're doing reading after reading for a line of eager, waiting querents, we quickly find a new meaning for the word "exhaustion." Exercising our ESP requires a lot of psychic energy, and if we don't take steps to keep our energy reserves well-stocked, we find ourselves worn and wan from those lengthier divination sessions. Try these easy tips to keep your psychic power flowing before, during, and after divination.

- *Nourish your body, nourish your mind.* Be sure to eat right and regularly to keep your psychic sense fit and active. On days you're doing divination, avoid eating heavy foods that can make you mentally and physically sluggish. Fruits, vegetables, non-meat proteins, and whole grains are key.

- *Quench your psychic thirst.* Drinking water during a divination session gives your vital force a boost and helps keep your psychic channels open and ready.

- *Plants are power.* Plants are living energy, and this energy can help strengthen your mind against psychic drain. Place plants around your divination area, and let their power fortify your own.

- *Another excuse to eat chocolate.* A little chocolate after a divination session will recharge your psyche and soothe your soul. Need I say more?

Secrets to Boosting Divination Accuracy

It's no coincidence that the best psychic readers are often the most experienced. After years of hands-on practice, we learn to read each querent not so much through the cards or runes we might use, but rather more directly, by picking up on the person's unique essence through no means other than our psychic intuition and common sense abilities to judge character. However, it doesn't have to take years to develop the ability to divine accurately. In fact, there are a few tricks and tips you can try that will give your divination skills a big push forward, instantly. Try this:

- *Get the whole story.* Whether using tarot, palmistry, runes, or another method, get an overview of the big picture given in the reading before discussing details with the querent.

- *What's the message?* Note your first impression of each querent. Ask yourself, "What is the message that this person most needs to hear right now?" and use that insight to help guide the reading in the right direction.

- *Psychometry helps.* Holding a personal, often-handled item belonging to the querent will help you pick up a lot of information about the person's past and current energetic state. Ask the querent for a piece of jewelry, keys, or other object, and hold it in your hand. Open your mind to the energetic sensations the object could be exuding. Keep the object with you throughout the reading to help clarify impressions.

- *Cross-check and double-check.* If you're unsure about the interpretation of a particular element of the reading, you can cross- and double-check your intuition by using the same or another divination tool, drawing a single card or rune, or gazing into a scrying surface with your best guess interpretation in mind. The impressions you receive will let you know whether or not you're on the right track.

- *Crystals and candles offer discreet help.* Candles and crystals can also be used to help clarify interpretations. Again, think of your best guess interpretation, then hold a clear quartz crystal in your hand or focus your gaze on a candle flame. If your interpretation is correct, the crystal will pulse strongly, and if you're using a candle, the flame will grow taller.

- *Just ask!* Most querents read like an open book if you're not afraid to ask questions. Encourage the querent to delve deeper by asking them questions implicated by the reading. For example, if a troubled relationship were to show up in the querent's tarot spread, you could give your interpretation, then ask the querent if there is more about the situation they would like to know. Let their answers guide you in giving practical, common sense answers of your own.

Divination for Goal-Setting Guidance

Here's how to use divination to help guide you when selecting goals for life, spirituality, and magick. See if you can figure out how you could use different types of divination for each goal-setting purpose.

Life Goals

Life goals are the things we want to accomplish personally, the story of our life as told by ourselves. This encompasses everything from relationships and families to careers and pastimes. One way to discover hidden life goals is with water scrying. Evaluate the types of visions you typically receive through this method of elemental divination. Is there a pattern that could clue you in on a potential life goal? For instance, if you often see visions of medical emergencies in your scrying basin, perhaps you should look in to going to medical school. If there doesn't seem to be a pattern to your visions, start a special scrying session by stating out loud that you would like to receive information about your specific life goals. After the session, investigate further any visions or impressions you received.

Spiritual Goals

Spiritual goals are those things we want to accomplish and experience spiritually, be it understanding and communion with deity, or achieving a state of inner peace and joy. One way to discover spiritual goals is with the tarot. Simply shuffle the deck as you focus on your spirituality. Ask the cards to reveal the story of your soul, what you need spiritually and your path to getting there. Do a complete reading using the Celtic Cross or a similar layout. The traditional attributions of each card's position will be a little different; just view the layout as a whole and interpret the cards in sequential order as you lay them out. What does the reading say about the general state of your spirituality? Are areas that need improvement indicated?

Magickal Goals

Magickal goals are the purpose and point of our magick, those things we hope to transform or manifest through spellwork. One way to narrow down magickal goals and determine if a particular spell could be successfully worked at the moment is with fire divination. Write your proposed goal on a piece of paper and place it in a fireproof dish. Set a corner of the paper on fire and watch what happens. If the writing on the paper is entirely consumed, it's a great time to try your spell; if the writing only partially burns, you might want to postpone the magick or reevaluate the spell goal.

Divination is Good for You!

Divination keeps our ESP in use and active, and when our psychic sense gets the benefit of a regular workout, it grows in leaps and bounds. Although the indications and information revealed to us through divination are by no means the destined, unalterable future, they do give us details about the current state of energies and the past patterns that led to these current states of energies. Through divination, we come to understand not only ourselves a little better, but we also gain insights into the spirituality and magick that come from a place much deeper than a little pack of cards or some lines on our palms.

EXERCISE

1. Of all the divination methods you've ever tried, which are you best at?
2. What forms of divination would you like to try or learn more about?
3. Do you feel that divination is accurate when employed to ascertain what the future will hold? How about when it's used to show what the future *may* hold? Why or why not?
4. What are some ways you could use divination for goal-setting guidance?
5. How does practicing divination improve our magickal abilities?

Taking It Further

Divination offers us a way to see into the past, present, and future, ascertaining the underlying patterns of energy on which our current reality is built. What other things could you find out with divination? Can you think of any mundane ways you could employ divination techniques to help you in practical matters of daily life?

Work on mastering at least one system of divination. It's a skill every witch should possess. If you're already a pro at tarot, try palmistry. If you're experienced with runes, tarot, palmistry, and other divination stand-bys, try unusual methods, or better yet, invent your own unique divination system.

In divination, the medium used is only a tool, a conduit for conveying information to the psychic sense. What other things in this world can you think of that serve us in this way?

10

Magickal Development

Whether you want fresh ideas to breathe more life into your craft or you're looking to improve your charms work or energy-raising skills, regular practice and variety will get you there. Through steady magickal development, we increase our power and refine our ability to impart our will in spellwork, and by exercising and evaluating our magickal abilities from several angles, we hone old skills and create new ones.

Learning new ways to develop magickal abilities and improve spellcasting techniques gives us a richer and broader perspective we can put to good use in designing our very own ways to do magick and our very own ways to keep those skills strong and sharp. Through your own insights and creativity, you can decide what works for you, custom-designing your own magickal workout and developing your power to cast spells better. Active development of magick skills is essential, so let's get to it.

Spellcasting's Four Essentials

Although your spells need not and should not follow a strict, prescribed structure, there are four essentials to successful spellcasting that can't be compromised. With these elements in place, you have great leeway in the design of your spells and the methods of your magick. Without these elements, magick won't work, even if you're using an ancient revered formula and following every instruction to a tee. Examining each essential step individually is beneficial. With a clearer understanding of what it takes to make magick work, you'll be better able to craft your own effective magickal methods.

Magickal Mindset

This is the number one essential ingredient in all successful spells. The magickal mindset is that state of mind in which we are confident in our ability to manipulate and direct energy through our consciousness, will, and intent. It is a psychically empowered mindset, an awareness of that which underlies and transcends the mundane. The conscious and subconscious minds are joined, and in this unified state the mind perceives and connects with the living tapestry of energy that is existence.

How to Achieve It

Every individual achieves and experiences the magickal mindset in a unique way. Just as your relationship with your mother is different from any other person's relationship with her, our personal connections to the fabric of life and our intimacy with nature and deity are one of a kind. You must find what turns *you* on and what puts *you* in the mental state to make magick happen.

You probably already have your own favorite ways to achieve the magickal mindset. However, exploring different methods allows us to switch it up a bit. Exploration opens up the opportunity for discovering a wider range of effective techniques and keeps our minds and our magick fresh while avoiding the rut of routine.

Methods you might want to employ to help you achieve the magickal mindset include meditation, self-hypnosis, conscious thought patterns, yoga, dance, music, drama, fasting, and chanting. Standing quietly and stretching out consciousness to greet the universe is a quick method of preparing the mind for magick that works for many busy witches. Other techniques include the consumption of consecrated food and drink, the use of psychoactive plant drugs such as cannabis, divine sage (*Salvia divinorum*), mushrooms, and peyote (these are traditional but often illegal methods that can lead to dangerous situations—research, be wise, and use caution!), altering awareness through images such as spirals and geometric patterns, and invoking higher mental states through the use of guises and costumes.

What Prevents It

Sometimes achieving a magickal mindset is not so much a matter of turning it on as it is a matter of not turning it off. Certain thought processes and actions block higher mental states and can thwart your chances for successfully working magick. These include:

Fear

Doubt

Mundane mental chatter

Egotism

Greed

Turn these off, and what's left is the magickal mindset.

Tip

If you like, you can establish a physical trigger to engage the magickal mindset instantaneously. Once you've got your mind in a ready state for magick, do something physical and unusual like touching your index finger to the center of your forehead or spinning around three times. Your mind will soon associate the physical trigger with the mental state you hope to achieve, and you'll be able to get into the magickal mindset quickly anytime simply by performing the associated physical action.

Magickal Mindset, Activate!

Let's be honest here. Quite a number of us have had the experience of a youthful exploration into psychedelics. For many who have, achieving the magickal mindset comes pretty naturally, as once we come to see enough of this underside/inside of reality, it becomes an ever-present aspect of our perception, always there and ready to be honed in on. Now I'm definitely not recommending you go take a bunch of LSD if that's something you haven't already done; I'm just saying that if you've never had the experience, it might be a little less easy to activate your magickal state of mind. Barring that, there are plenty of safe and legal ways to transcend the mundane and take a journey into mystical territory, ways that don't require you to know an old-school Deadhead, though that's hardly ever a bad idea (really, they're nice)!

For those on the straight and narrow looking to broaden their horizons and gain a whole new perspective on reality, there are a number of techniques to try. Traditional sweat lodge experiences are often effective in taking consciousness into an altered state of awareness. If that doesn't work or isn't your style, you might try extensive drumming, beating on a hand drum for hours on end. For many, practicing self-hypnosis or astral projection does the trick. If you're the quiet type, go with it and try spending several days without speaking at all; it will definitely reset your thought patterns and bring to light aspects of reality you might not have noticed before.

Exposure to art is another way to become aware of different layers of reality. Check out art exhibits, listen to a variety of music, buy lots of books and read them. You never know when or where you'll see, hear, or read that little something that triggers a whole chain reaction of magickal awareness and understanding.

If you find yourself having difficulty feeling magickal and it's hard for you to get into a state of mind conducive for spellwork, experiment with different ideas and keep trying. Don't let this uppermost, mundane, hectic, and demanding level of reality get the better of you! Times like this are when we know an actively sought-out mystical journey is called for; choose your vehicle and travel safely.

EXERCISE TO CONNECT TO MAGICKAL POWER

Ideally, the witch can sense and connect to the magickal force even in the most chaotic of circumstances. However, it's a skill that must be developed, and often practitioners find that it is in moments of peaceful solitude and solitary practice that we make our greatest leaps forward into new awareness and greater understanding of magick's most essential mysteries. When we have time, it's beneficial to connect with the energies we work with in magick without asking for anything, without changing the energy in any way, without casting any charms or spells. Taking a moment to just "hang out" with magickal power, letting yourself be fully immersed in it, creates an opportunity for these forces and energies to communicate information, in effect inviting magickal power to cast a spell on *you!*

One way of connecting to the magickal force starts with locating it within yourself. Sit alone outside, relax in a bath, lay down in the dark, frolic in the forest, or do whatever else most readily allows you to tune out and just be. Turn off as much of you as possible, taking a break from the body and the mundane mind and casting aside for a moment your obligation to "be you" and operate the physical form, personality, and identity that contains you. What is left? Can you sense this in your surrounding environment, also? With "you" turned off, what's left in you is magickal power, and this same power can be found in everything.

Energy Raising

In order to cast a spell, energy must first be raised or gathered, just as the ingredients must first be obtained before making a delicious cake. Energy raising is the calling together or gathering of the forces we work with in magick, the magickal power that lies within and throughout everything. Energy is gathered and amplified to a fever pitch, putting it in a state where it can be manipulated and coded with information to cause it to do what we like.

How to Do It

You're probably adept at raising energy; after all, it's one of the basic steps of magick. But are there sources of energy you might be missing out on? Are you making the most out of all the resources available to you? The more energy behind it, the more powerful the magick, and it pays to gather as much energy as you possibly can from wherever you can to use in your spells. Energy can be gathered from both internal and external sources, from our own inner power as well as from the natural world and deity. Anything considered a "higher power," and anything seen to contain such power, can be tapped into, providing a useful source of energy for spellwork.

There are infinite aspects of the living energy and the magickal power that comprises it, and which aspects you choose to call on for your magick is entirely a matter of personal preference. However, experimenting with different energy sources is beneficial, as it gives you access to a wider pool of magickal power. Many witches invoke the elements, simply sensing and connecting to the essences of earth, air, fire, water, and spirit and calling these forces forth through consciousness and intent. Nature spirits have a reputation for being particularly helpful. Some magickal practitioners call on multiple aspects of deity, such as god and goddess, or on one all-encompassing deity. Still others call on spirits of loved ones who have passed on. You can also gather energy for spells through the use of plants, stones, crystals, candles, art, music, movement, symbols, sounds, sensations, numbers, words, and colors that have energetic vibrations complementary to your magical goal. You may even elect to gather up your own energy before a magickal rite, using heightened awareness to pump up your personal power. The key to more potent magick is to gather absolutely all the helpful and willing energy you can summon.

What Prevents It

When we're unable to gather and raise energy, it's a sure sign of a spiritual disconnect. Either we have no real connection to or understanding of the source from which we're hoping to draw magickal power, or else we are simply shut off psychically from communicating with these forces because we failed to reach a magickal mindset beforehand. We're able to raise energy much better when we know our energy sources intimately and when we take the time to really get into our magick.

Tip

Once you've gathered energy, make the most of it: absorb the energy into your core and let it pulsate throughout your entire being, amplifying the energy you have summoned with the power of your own spirit. Picture the energy as a vivid light, colored in tune with your aim, and sense the energy growing stronger and brighter as you infuse it with your own spiritual power. Focus on your own inner essence that corresponds with your goal, and let this essence spread throughout your body and throughout the energy you have gathered. Drumming, dancing, running, jumping, or chanting might enhance your ability to amplify energy. When the energy feels as pure and bright as it can possibly be, your body will tingle. This is the time to move on to the next step.

Energy Discerning Exercise

If you want to know how well you're able to accurately sense the exact energies you're trying to connect with in magick and also improve your ability to do so, try this. For this exercise you'll need a partner, someone whose skills in the magickal arts you can trust. Have your partner prepare two quartz crystals by charging each one with a distinct vibration. One could be set with a negative vibe, the other with a positive. Now hold the crystals in your own hands and see if you can tell them apart. Your partner will then tell you whether or not you're correct. Make a note of it.

If your results are consistently less than encouraging, try the exercise with a different person. Sometimes our energies just don't click with certain individuals, which can lead to a misleadingly low success rate in tests like this.

Energy Coding

Once energy is gathered, it is coded and programmed to carry out its specific magickal purpose. The energy is imprinted with information that sets it into a pattern that is likely to produce the desired change. Energy coding is the step in spellwork where one or more of magick's seven functions are carried out.

How to Do It

Assuming you've cast a spell before, you understand how to code energy: you simply imprint it with your will and intent. Although this can be accomplished in countless ways, we tend to go with the familiar and use the same techniques again and again, be it candle magick, herb magick, spoken words, or Haitian Voudou. When we're adept at many methods of energy coding, our spellwork becomes more precise and effective. Further, gaining a new perspective on methods of energy coding you're already familiar with will give you greater knowledge of the process so that you'll understand what is really going on during each step when you cast a spell. Let's take a look at some ways to code energy:

Solely Mentally

Energy can be coded using nothing but your own mental power, a.k.a. magickal power in the brain. To do this, contemplate the true essence of your aim. For instance, if you're working a spell to bring monetary gain, think of increase and attraction, of giving and sharing, of abundance, opportunity, and wealth. You must find this same essence in the energies you have gathered, and call it forth. Start by noticing the diversity and nuances of the vibrational patterns of energy within you and surrounding you. Once you've identified the vibration most similar to that of your magickal goal, focus on it and think of that vibration growing in strength, so that all the gathered energy is soon pulsating with this same essence. The energy has now been imprinted with the information it needs to tell it what to do; by mentally adjusting the vibrations, you have installed an energetic code, preparing the magickal power to be released as your spell.

Likewise, you can code energy through simple visualization, seeing in your mind's eye the desired outcome of your magick. For example, with a love spell, you could code the energy by seeing yourself looking totally in love and feeling completely loved. Always see your goal as if it has already been attained. Believe, and try to experience how it will feel to have your desire fulfilled. See your desired outcome clearly, but keep in mind that it may come about in a different way than you anticipate. Have faith in destiny to get it right, and don't worry about the particulars. The more vividly and confidently you can imagine having acquired your aim, the more completely will the energy be coded and the more successful will your magick be in making your wishes reality.

Imitative Actions

Another way energy is coded for spellwork is through imitative actions, otherwise known as imitative magick. We've all heard the phrase, "As above, so below"; this idea is the foundation of energy coding through imitation. What's true is true on all levels: the same physical and magickal laws governing a grain of dirt will apply also to a giant heap of dirt, and even to the universe at large. The magickal concept here is that if you can cause a change in the one grain of dirt, then the dirt heap, and the universe, will experience that change as well.

The items, actions, and symbols we use in magick are energetically connected to all other levels of reality with the same or similar vibration, and by manipulating these magickal trappings, we can code the associated energy on all levels of its existence. For example, if the passion-inducing property of patchouli is called forth into action and told to fetch you a new lover, then the passion-inducing energies that exist throughout the universe will likewise be called into duty. By imitating on a small scale what we wish to happen on a large scale, we code the energy at both a microcosmic and macrocosmic level.

Here's an example of coding energy through imitative magick. Suppose you want to acquire a wonderful new car. One way you could code the energy for this spell would be to adapt a Barbie or Ken doll to look more like you, writing your name on it, styling the hair, changing the clothes, etc., and then sitting this now-you doll in Barbie's toy Corvette. By doing so, you've coded the energy right there in front of you and throughout the universe at large with the information that you are to have a new car, and you did it all from your present position.

Image Magick

Image magick, a specific type of imitative magick, is another way to code magickal energy. You simply create an image of what you wish to manifest, illustrating exactly what you want the energy to do. For example, to code energy in a way that will lead to you finding a lost possession, you could draw a picture of yourself with the lost item in your hand, holding it up triumphantly.

Image magick works on the same principles that apply to other types of imitative magick. By creating from our own little sphere of reality a symbol of what we want our magick to do, we imprint the associated energies with a new pattern that will resonate throughout all corresponding levels of reality.

Web Weaving

Web weaving is yet another way to code energy. Here, you forge energetic connections that didn't previously exist and weave the energy you wish to affect into the energies you have readily available. For example, say your magickal goal is to cause the United Nations to take a particular action. Chances are, you don't have any personal experience with the UN and will therefore find it extremely difficult to identify or access the energetic essence of this organization. If you can find some common ground, though, however vague, you can use that common ground to connect to the broader energies you want to code. For instance, the members of the UN sit behind a long table. You might not know the UN, but you know all about tables. You could work your spell to affect the UN by coding the energy of your own table, thereby affecting the energy in tables everywhere, including the one at the UN! You would simply connect with the energy of your own table and then stretch out your consciousness to access the energy of tables worldwide. You could state out loud if you like that your own table is now connected to all tables in existence. Then, when you affect a change in the energy of the table in front of you, the same change will take place in all other tables. This includes the energy of the table at the UN, which will be coded to suit your purpose and will in turn affect the members that sit behind it.

What Prevents It

Proper energy coding is prevented when we fail to establish a connection or when the code we are attempting to impart is vague or dysfunctional. Just as a computer program won't work right if there is a bug or error in the code, so too will magick fail if the energy is coded improperly. To ensure correct and complete energy coding, commit to the magick and give it your full consciousness, will, and intent. Make sure the pattern you're wishing to impress on the energies you're working with is the right one for the job and that you're not overlooking some major thing that could thwart it all. Proper planning and full commitment are the keys to successful energy coding.

Tip

Code the energy when the power is at its height, raised to an intense and radiant vibration. If you try to code the energy at a moment when your power has waned or when your visualization has gotten cloudy, your magick will be less effective. When magickal power has been raised to its fullest, a crystal clear idea has been formed in your mind, and a strong sense of what you want to achieve is in your heart, this is the exact moment in which to code the energy to ensure spellcasting success.

ENERGY CODING EXERCISE

This exercise tests and strengthens your ability to effectively manipulate magickal energies. Basically, you will attempt to affect the energy of a substance or item and then check to see if it actually worked. Here's how.

Start with something that has readily available energy that takes well to manipulation, such as rosemary or basil. Create two identical dishes of the herb, making a small mark on the underside of one of the bowls. Now code the energies of each dish separately and distinctly. For instance, with the rosemary, you could empower one dish of the herb to bring out healing energies, and the other to bring out loving energies, both properties being inherent qualities in the plant that can be magnified to "take over" the vibrations throughout the entire dish of herb. With the basil, you could code one dish to the vibration of wealth, while the other dish is coded to match the essence of protection. Once you've imparted the magick, check your results. Change the position of the dishes or get a friend to rearrange them so you won't know which is which. Now touch each dish of herb and see if you can distinguish them. Can you? If you can't tell, ask a witchy-minded friend to try; it might be that you can code energy just fine but have trouble sensing those distinctions once they're cast. Once you achieve a pretty good success rate with the herbs, try doing the experiment with something more difficult to manipulate, such as sand, granite, or coins. Keep note of your results and keep trying to improve your average. However good we are, we can all get better, and with regular practice we're rewarded with better spellcasting abilities!

Releasing the Magick

Once the energy is coded and the spell has been woven, it's time to release the magick to do its work. This is the actual casting of the spell, when the energies that are now imprinted with your goal are released and activated. Releasing the energy of a spell is a way of magickally expressing the sentiment, "It is done. Now go get to it!"

How to Do It

Although the details of the experience are unique to each of us, we all release the energy of a spell in basically the same way: we simply will it to be so. We consciously use our intent and our will to send the energy of a spell exactly where it needs to go to do its work. We feel the energy flow out of us, maybe visualizing a current of magickal power coursing out into the wider world.

One effective method of releasing the energy of a spell starts by taking within yourself all the gathered coded energy that is imprinted with your goal, feeling your body pulsate with the energy's luminous charge. Then concentrate this magickal power all into your fingertips, into the very tip of your wand or ritual knife if you're using one, or to a point right behind your eyes. Once all the magickal energy in your body is gathered at this one place, promptly and deliberately release it, willing it to burst powerfully into the wider universe in a rush to tweak circumstances into your favor.

You can direct the release of energy more specifically if you like, for instance, sending it into an object to charm it with magickal properties, sending it into a person in need of healing or help, or directing it in a spiral motion around yourself to affect a personal transformation.

What Prevents It

We have trouble releasing the energy of a spell when we doubt our ability to do so, or when we don't finish the job completely and fail to release quite all of the magick.

As humans, we are blessed with the inherent ability to manipulate and direct energy through our own magickal power, and we need to give it our all and really believe in it when we use this power. Know you can do it, and really strive to release absolutely all the energy of your spell, staying in tune with your body so you can tell whether or not you're still harboring some of the magick. Many witches find they release energy more fully and easily if a physical action accompanies it, such as flicking the wand, wiggling one's fingers, or clapping.

Tip

If you're working a spell aimed at a particular person or place, you can more successfully release the magickal energy to hit its target by specifically identifying that target. Try stating out loud at the moment of your spell's release the name or another identifying characteristic of whom or to where your spell is directed. Doing so will help the magick reach its destination more quickly and directly.

Energy-Release Exercise

Want to challenge and improve your ability to carry out magick's fourth essential, the step when the energy of a spell is released? Here's an activity to help you do just that.

For this exercise, you'll need three magick beans. Seriously. Well, they don't have to be magick to start with—any three virtually identical dried beans will do! Start by holding one of the beans in your hand and charging it up to a specific magickal vibration of your choice, coding the energy of the bean to an essence that you feel confident in conjuring. Now touch this bean to the other beans, directing the coded energy of the first bean into the other two. Then mix them all in your hand until you can't tell which one is the original bean. Next, hold each bean one at a time, noting whether or not it feels magickally charged. If you've done the exercise successfully, you should now have two charged beans and one uncharged bean— the original bean should be back to its normal mundane bean self, while the other two should now feel like the first bean did right after you charged it up. Did it work? Does only one bean feel completely devoid of the magick you cast? If so, it worked! If not, take down the details of your observations.

Does one bean feel like it still has a little power in it, weaker than the other two beans but still noticeable? This indicates that you did not release the coded energy completely but rather left some behind in the original bean. Does only one bean feel charged? If so, it indicates either that the attempt was not at all successful and that the energy remained in the original bean, or that you managed to successfully cast the magick into one of the secondary beans but not into the other one. Either way, you'll know to keep trying.

Practicing and testing our ability to release magickal energy gives us a giant leg up in our spellcasting. We know where we stand when it comes to energy/spell release, and we know which skills we've got in abundance and which we need to hone. We know when we've failed and we quickly learn to get it right more often.

Tips for Better Wand Usage

A big part of your magickal development is mastering the basics. Although you might not be especially keen on them, magick wands are undoubtedly the quintessential witch emblem. Even if you don't plan on using one regularly, it's a good idea to know how to if you really want to be a well-rounded witch. Unfortunately, most magick wands don't come with an instruction manual. It's up to us to refine our techniques to make best use of this handy implement. Here's a quick primer/refresher course in the successful use of wands:

When gathering energy for your magick, in general, you'll want to channel it down through your wand tip and into your body. The exception is when the wand itself is designed to do the coding of energy, for instance a wand made specifically to transform any energy it absorbs into psychic visions that will be stored in the wand and manifested whenever you choose to release them. If that's the case, direct the energy as you're gathering it into the wand, leaving it right there in the wand instead of pulling it down into your body.

Once the energy has been coded, whether in your body or in your wand, when it is time to release the magickal energy, send it back through your wand, concentrating it all in the tip. To release the spell, flick, wave, or tap the wand.

You can refine your wand movements to cast your magick more effectively. For instance, if you are empowering or otherwise enchanting an object, tap it with the wand to send the magick into it. For spells designed to attract something to you, such as a spell to bring more opportunity into your life, a smooth waving motion is most effective. For charms, a quick swish or flick is best, while for defensive magick, a jab or sharp slashing movement works best. If your magick is intended to stop something in its tracks or otherwise bring an end or delay to a matter, point the wand tip straight down and bring it sharply toward the earth. Practice and experiment to find what works best, and you'll learn to hone your wand usage to personal perfection.

Rituals, Charms, Spells: What's Your Pleasure?

After a while, most of us begin to settle in to a particular aspect of the magickal arts, be it rituals, charms, or spellwork. Making sure we do all three in fair measure brings balance and variety to our magickal practice and aids in our overall development as well-rounded witches.

Perhaps mainly due to the desire of writers (including me!) to not use the same words again and again in their writing, the terms "rituals," "spells," and "charms" are often used interchangeably, all taken to mean simply "a magickal act." However, the three are quite different. Knowing exactly what each type of magickal working is and does helps us identify what magick would be best in a given situation. And making sure we are well practiced in this great trinity of the magickal arts improves our ability to successfully do magick in any situation. Let's take a look at each one in turn.

Rituals

Rituals are at the core of the witch's spirituality and magickal craft; these are the ceremonies and symbolic acts and traditions we carry out in reverence and celebration of our personal concepts of deity or what we consider to be higher powers or spiritual/magickal forces. Just as you might not feel like helping a friend who always forgets your birthday, the forces that can aid us in magick might not be too motivated to rush to our rescue if the only time we pay attention is when we're asking a favor.

Rituals offer us a way to show we care, a way to express the fact that we're not just in it for the magick! We want real spiritual evolution, we want real connections to nature and the higher powers, and we want to use magick in a spiritually guided magnificent way. Performing a ritual is like saying thanks and leaving a tip for the server at the restaurant—it's polite and expected.

Many witches perform rituals in honor of the moon phases or seasonal cycles, typically calling on and honoring any deities or forces associated and paying respect and reverence in words or actions. Usually a pleasant environment is created through candles and incense, and perhaps music or song is added. Theatrical scenes or other symbolic actions might be performed to illustrate and connect with the great mysteries of nature and deity. Offerings are sometimes left— wine, fruit, nuts, flowers, coins, a drop of one's own blood, or a small lock of one's own hair are some of the sacrifices often given.

Of course, the form and frequency of your rituals is something to decide for yourself. It really doesn't matter if the ritual is elaborate or simple, traditional or contemporary, prescribed or one of your own totally one-of-a-kind creations. Many of us are pressed for time and perpetually drained of energy; we just can't really commit to having all-out rituals every month. Still, a ritual can be as easy as lighting a candle and saying thanks—it doesn't have to take a lot of time to show your gratitude. The important thing is to do some sort of ritual regularly, be it a practical five-minute ritual every morning or an intricate hour-long ritual every full moon. If you've neglected your rituals, it's time to reconnect.

Charms

Charms are bits of magick that work instantly. Basically a flash of magickal power that does its duty immediately upon release, a charm is quicker to perform and acts more quickly than a spell. When a charm is cast, magick's four essentials are carried out automatically all in an instant, without the practitioner having to consciously perform each step.

Mastering charms is beneficial because magick is so often needed in the moment. We often find ourselves in situations where we need to affect something right there in the now, situations that will be beyond repair if we wait until we get home and drag out every magickal tool and trapping we own. If we practice our charms work regularly, we stay in prime shape to use those skills in the heat of the moment, and we're able to cast fast-acting magick with immediate results.

Above all, a charm is fast and cuts right to the chase. Only with full commitment to the act and sincere belief in the magick can the witch cast a charm successfully. One way to cast a charm is to quickly visualize exactly what you want to happen and state it forcibly in words or actions as you send out a blast of magickal power, your consciousness, will, and intent all rolled into one and projected outward with intensity. Many witches like to flick a wand or wave their hand or perform a similar action to aid in the fast and easy release of the charm, while others simply flash their eyes or say an appropriate word of power.

Let's look at an example to illustrate just how and why a charm might be cast. Suppose you get ready to leave for work, and you find your car won't start. Sure, you could take the time to work an elaborate spell to unclog your oil line or reset the electrical system, but it would take a lot of time to not only cast that spell but to have it actually work and do its duty, too. Spells are slower-acting than charms. The clock is ticking, and you're late. You simply don't have time for a spell, but you know better than to fret. You decide to cast a charm instead. Visualizing the car starting, hearing in your mind the sound of the engine revving and purring, you send a blast of magickal power out of your eyes and directly at the ignition as you firmly say, "Start!" The engine catches, and you're off to the office. Charms to the rescue!

Of course, there are countless ways to cast charms, and as the process is so brief, it's hard to grasp the particulars without actual experience. If you haven't done so already, experiment and determine what might be your own best method.

Charms aren't the place for variety. We want them to work and we want them to work fast, so find your most effective technique and for the most part, stick to it. It's good to practice different methods to broaden your skills, but try that at your leisure and not when a charm is urgently needed.

Knowing how to cast charms successfully is a basic and integral skill in the magickal arts. It pays to practice and get really good at it, as the witch whose charms work is excellent can often take command in even the most chaotic of circumstances. Besides, casting charms is fun! Try casting a charm to remove a tough spot when you're washing dishes, try to trick that falling bowl of cereal into landing upright, attempt to charm that totally attractive stranger into accidentally dropping their parcels right beside you. Be inspired, and give it a try. Using charms regularly will add magick to your life, and a life full of magick never gets dull.

Spells

A spell is a more involved form of magick, where each step of the magick is carried out consciously and often with accompanying action. Whereas in a charm you do all the gathering, coding, and releasing of energy all in a second, a spell takes time. It doesn't have to take a lot of time, but it does take longer than casting a charm. Spells also typically take a little while to reach full fruition, leaving a waiting period of anywhere from several hours to a whole year to bring you the results you seek. However, the wait is worth it, as spells can do things charms can't. Though the casting process is more complex and though it takes more time to reap the harvest, spells are farther reaching and longer lasting than charms. With spells you can use magick intricately and precisely to manifest what's desired on a broader scope, reworking major patterns underlying reality to create wide, multi-level changes.

For example, suppose you want to successfully create a new and profitable career path for yourself. Obviously, a quick charm isn't going to do the trick this time. A charm could certainly get your job application to the top of the stack, a charm could maybe even land you an impromptu interview, but charms don't linger around long enough to produce the substantial and long-term results you would be going for in this particular situation. A spell would be what's called for.

A witch might cast such a spell by beginning with a nice long bath to relax followed by some drumming to ready the mind for magick. After that, the energy for the magick is gathered. The Horned God or another deity that represents power and authority might be summoned, or perhaps a jade stone, which has an energetic essence that corresponds to skill, destiny, and leadership, is placed on the altar to add its energies to the spell. The witch might then flatten out a piece of clay and into this carve words or symbols that express the ultimate desired career path and the fulfillment of the heart's most ambitious hopes and dreams. In this way, the witch codes the gathered energy to manifest the opportunities and circumstances that will lead to the coveted occupation. Finally, when the energy is fully programmed and running at full power, the witch taps the clay emblem with her fingertips and sends the magickal energy coursing into it. She now has a ready talisman to wear or carry that is sure to weave its magick in her career sphere for years to come.

Of course, a spell to do this exact same thing could be done in a completely different manner using completely different tools and mediums. But although each spell is different on the surface, remember that at the core, all spells are cast in essentially the same way. Simply carry out each of magick's four essentials consciously: first getting yourself into a magickal mindset, next gathering energy from any power sources you choose, then coding the gathered energy completely and consciously in whatever way you like, and finally releasing the energy to actually cast the spell.

Most likely, you already cast spells fairly often. But are you really using your spellcasting powers to the fullest? Are you trying new things while retaining your ability to use your old standby techniques? Are you casting a variety of spells in a variety of ways regularly, keeping your skills sharp and getting better and better with each bit of magick you perform? Mastering this basic isn't enough. We need to continuously strive to take our ability to cast spells to the next level if we really want to maintain our magickal momentum.

Spellcasting is what witches do. It's not the biggest thing or the only important thing, but it is an exceedingly powerful tool to use in the creation of a more positive world and a more pleasant existence. There's plenty of magickal work to do and not enough of us are doing it. You're not alone, so get to it! The pay might not be the greatest, but the benefits are outstanding!

Daily Practice Keeps It Going

Those of us who practice some sort of magick daily find that doing so keeps our magickal power strong. When we're well practiced and magickal processes are fresh in our minds, we can carry out any magick quite simply. On the other hand, if we only cast spells a few times a year or so, we run the risk of letting our skills get rusty. If we're not careful to increase the frequency of our magickal practice when we notice this happening, we can reach a point where it is extremely difficult and takes the utmost concentration and determination to perform even basic spells that were once a breeze. This is often what has happened to witches who feel they have "lost their magick." With daily practice, greater magickal power is found.

Magickal Improvisation

Have you ever been to an improv theater, where the actors on the stage create the scene right then and there from audience cues and whatever props are on hand? Improvisation is a great way for actors to improve their acting skills, and it's also a great way for witches to improve their spellcasting skills! Magickal improvisation is the process of creating a spell in the moment, any moment, using whatever tools and ingredients happen to be available at that time. Practicing this skill increases our versatility and challenges our abilities. When we're able to design and cast a spell in virtually any circumstance, then those spells we cast when we do have the luxury of time and a decent stock of magickal ingredients will really pack a punch. Versatility makes the witch, and practicing magickal improvisation is a great way to develop it.

Try this. Throughout your day, whether that finds you in your kitchen, in school, at the office, at the park, or even at a fast food restaurant, take a moment to look around you and see what's available that you could use magickally. Pick a few spell goals and see if you can come up with a way to cast each one. For example, you might be at a diner and decide to craft a protection charm. Look around. Are there salt and pepper on the table, spices that are great for banishing and protection magick? Might there even be some hot sauce to add an extra dash of defensive power to your charm? Could you make use of the knife or fork somehow? See what you can come up with.

Looking at another example, suppose you were at the office, and you want to try to improvise a love spell. There are no herbs, no oils, no candles…what can you do? Well, there are probably paper and a pen available; why not cast a written charm, perhaps even creating a word talisman? Or maybe you could use water from the water cooler to create a love potion. You could even make use of the copy machine, drawing an image that invokes love and making duplicates of it in a bit of imitative multiplication magick.

Use what you've got and fill in the blanks; remember that tools and ingredients are extras and are not required. A skilled witch can make do with whatever is available, even if what's available is absolutely nothing.

Experiment!

"You never know what you can do until you try": a cliché that actually rings quite true. Only through experimentation and practice will you discover your limits, and you must know your limits in order to break through them. Many people feel unsure about their magickal skills, and are hesitant to try spells they suspect might be too complex, too ambitious, or too over the top. This is nonsense. Aim high. You are hereby certified to try whatever magick you like, however you like; consider yourself a fully qualified witch or wizard. Try working magick to accomplish real miracles and see what happens. See if you can get two warring nations to sign a peace treaty, see if you can put out a forest fire, see if you can reduce violent crime in your city, see if you can bring an endangered species back from the brink. There is plenty such work to do, and it will take plenty of us working on both a magickal and a mundane level to make it happen. So give it a try; do your part. You'll be surprised by your success and educated by your failures. If you truly want to know what all your magick can accomplish, there's only one way to find out—attempt it.

Design Your Own Magickal Workout

If you're really willing to put in the practice and study to further your education in the arts of magick as much as you can, try challenging yourself with a magickal workout of your own design. Just four choices to make and you'll have created your own system for making sure your magick grows stronger by the day. Here's what you'll need to decide:

Frequency

Will it work for you to have a set schedule of workout days, or will you do it when you can, perhaps committing to exercising your magickal powers once or twice a month, whenever time allows? Decide what works. Although a magickal workout is not like a gym workout, it's the same in that if it's convenient, we're much more likely to actually do it.

Target Skills

Are there particular magick skills you want to develop or improve? Do you want to increase your ESP? Would you like to learn more about astrology or plant identification? Is there a certain branch of magick you would like to learn more about? Choose three skills you want to focus on building right now. These target skills should change fairly regularly, for variety and a fuller education.

Exercises

What activities will you do to strengthen these target skills? Will you read books? Will you meditate? Will you try any of the exercises suggested in this chapter? For each workout session, challenge yourself to design or choose at least three different activities you could do to boost your magickal prowess in each of your target skills, then do them.

The Main Magick

In addition to exercises for refining various aspects of magickal skill, try making all-out magick a part of your regular workout, too, performing a complete spell, charm, or ritual for whatever purpose you choose.

Tip

If you find yourself running out of energy during a magickal workout, take a break—eat some dark chocolate, drink some water, or perform some quick, simple task. You'll be rejuvenated and able to get back to your exercises promptly.

Some days, however, we're simply out of steam and no amount of chocolate will fix it, no matter how delicious. On days like this, it's best to just take it easy. If you are disciplined and diligent about doing a daily magickal workout, don't stress if you need or want to skip it sometimes. We all need a day off now and then, so take one!

EXERCISE

1. What do you feel are the essential steps in the magickal process?
2. Can you think of at least three different ways you could carry out each of these steps?
3. Do you have more of a flair for charms or for spells?
4. Is there a bit of experimental magick floating within your head that you would like to try? What is it?
5. What are three things you would like to do to increase your magickal abilities?

Taking It Further

By pursuing a steady course of magickal development, we find the road forward into better spellcasting. Think about what this really means to you. What paths will you traverse? Are you heading for a particular destination, or enjoying a nice walkabout and seeing where adventure finds you? Decide where and how far you want to go in your magickal development, right now. Though your path might twist and turn, having a clear goal in mind and the motivation to pursue it always helps in getting there.

11

Magickal Cooking:
From Chore to Charming

These days, kitchen witchery and more folky types of spellwork are sometimes perceived to be lesser, lower forms of magick. In reality, nothing could be further from the truth. Common practices of common folks using practical, everyday magick to produce desired change are at the very heart of our magickal history. This type of spellwork has indeed been a preserving force in magick, as folk traditions are passed from generation to generation and are adapted to grow with the times, made practical for each practitioner based on what is possible for each practitioner. One such tradition is magickal cooking, a powerful form of spellwork that is perfect for the busy or frazzled. Daily meal preparation can be a bit of a drag, but when you transform it into a spellcasting, your time spent in the kitchen becomes a convenient way to increase your magickal power and expand your skills. Even when our everyday obligations don't leave us much time for all-out spells and rituals, we can still squeeze some magick into our daily cooking, adding power to our meals, creativity and flexibility to our spellcrafting, and spice to our lives.

Intent: Your Secret Ingredient

Every great cook has a secret ingredient. For the magickal cook, that ingredient is intent. From choosing and purchasing foods to slicing and stirring, each step of the cooking process must be carried out with magickal intent. Food possesses inherent magickal qualities, and when cooked with intent, the natural power of food is magnified. Once we learn to work with this power, our meals become a handy medium for housing charms, spells, and other enchantments that can be activated in a flash through the simple act of eating. So let's get to it!

Choosing Ingredients

Choose ingredients with magickal attributes and associations in mind. Think about your intent. What effect do you want the food to produce? Once you decide, find an ingredient with that attribute and consider including it in your recipe. You can also do this the other way around, looking in your cupboard to see what you already have on hand, looking up the magickal attributes of those ingredients, and then seeing what you can make out of them. (Anyone adept at making what I call "no groceries in the house to speak of casserole" will be quite skilled in this!)

If you haven't yet developed your own system of magickal attributes, never fear. You can take suggestions from the ingredient correspondences provided in this chapter, and consult more extensive herbals, as well, while you work on discovering your own feelings about magickal foods. Explore various ingredients. Touch them, smell them, taste them, sense their energies. What does the ingredient feel like to you? What does it make you think of? Do you agree with the attributes ascribed to the ingredient in your favorite herbal? Is the ingredient's energy light and airy, or heavy and strong? Is it mysterious and dreamy? Calming? Fiery? Take note of your impressions, and you'll soon have a very reliable personal cookbook of shadows.

Not every ingredient in your recipe needs to be magickally attuned. Use your imagination; if a particular food seems to have qualities suited to your magick, go for it!

To get the ideas flowing, here are just a few "power ingredients" that are common, versatile, very magickal, and can be used in many types of food:

- *Garlic:* protection, defense, strength, energy, banishing, health, courage
- *Rice:* health, prosperity
- *Rosemary:* health, happiness, spirit communication, psychic awareness, peace, love, prosperity, passion, good luck, protection, purification, success
- *Salt:* success, happiness, prosperity, strength, banishing, honesty, energy, purification, defense, protection
- *Wheat:* strength, success, growth, energy, stability, peace

Now let's look at the other aspects of adding intent to your cooking.

Purchasing Ingredients

Magickal intent can also be incorporated when shopping for groceries. When witches harvest wild herbs to use in magick, we say thanks, expressing gratitude to the earth for the gift of the herbs. In contrast, the food we buy in grocery stores was likely pulled from the earth in a very unceremonious fashion, processed (often with chemicals), stuffed into packaging, crammed into a semi-truck, and shipped to market. Not exactly magickal. It's never too late to show appreciation, though, and doing so will rev up the power of the food and give it fresh energy.

When you grab food off the shelves at the grocery store, whisper under your breath, or say inside your head, words that express gratitude to the earth for the blessing of food. If you like, lightly tap the product three times with your fingertips before you pick it up. Shopping with magickal intent makes your ingredients more powerful, infusing them from the get-go with the energetic intention that they will be used for a special purpose. Of course, if you have the option, it makes sense to show at local farmer's markets, where you're likely to find foods that have retained more of their natural charge. Powerful ingredients make powerful food, and powerful food makes powerful magick.

Empowering Your Ingredients

Once you get your ingredients home, you'll need to further empower them with the specific intent of your magick. Each ingredient has many qualities and characteristics, and it's up to you to bring out the best, to bring to the forefront the particular magickal attribute you desire for your spell. Basil, for instance, contains an energetic vibration that is useful in love spells, and it also has an energetic vibration that is useful in prosperity charms. If you're making money-bringing food, you'll want to empower your basil so that its prosperity energy is prominent and amplified.

Touch the ingredient, sense its energies, and do what you can to magnify the quality that matches your magickal intent. In the basil example, for instance, you could simply say out loud, "I call on the prosperity energy in this basil to come forth and be amplified." Or you could empower it by visualizing the basil pulsing and glowing with an energy of prosperity and abundance, and see this light as growing in intensity and size. Another method is to draw a symbol (or use a rune or a Tarot card) that represents the quality in the ingredient that you wish to magnify. Place the ingredient on top of the symbol until it feels infused with the desired energy. (You might want to call out, "Absorb this!" as you place the ingredient on the symbol.) There are many, many ways to empower ingredients. Try different methods; the more ways you have of doing something, the more your magickal prowess increases. Once you've empowered your ingredients, it's time to get down to the business of magickal cooking.

Magickal Flour Sifting

If you enjoy baking and you like using a flour sifter, try making it a magickal experience. You can break up clumps in the flour as well as in your own life as you turn that little metal handle. Put the flour in the sifter, and gaze down into it. Think of anything that troubles you, any bad habits, any negative influences, habitual worries, anything that you wish to sift out of your life. Send these thoughts into the flour. As you work the sifter, imagine the negative things in your life being sorted out and strained out as the flour moves through the wire screen. You can tailor the sifting process to suit the intent of your magickal cooking. For instance, if you're making bread to magnify romantic passion, you could put your inhibitions into the flour to be sifted out. If you're baking cookies to amplify your leadership qualities, put your shyness and insecurities into the sifter. Once you've sifted through the flour, shake the empty sifter upside down and dispel the energetic trash by saying something like, "Away! Neutralize!" See the sifted flour as pure; notice the absence of the energies you sifted out.

Cut It Out

A similar exercise can be performed while chopping ingredients. Hold the knife in your hand and focus your thoughts on the things you wish to cut out of your life. As you make each cut, imagine that you are slicing through the energies you want to be rid of. See the blade pushing those unwanted energies out and away. If you like, you can state your intent with each slice you make, saying something such as, "I'm cutting through the unnecessary. I'm cutting out the negative."

Combining Ingredients

If possible, choose a mixing bowl whose color or form reflects the intent of the magickal food you're cooking. A glass bowl would be good for a meal to bring clarity. A pink bowl would be good for a romance food. A square dish would be good for a recipe to bring structure, order, decrease, or boundaries, while a round dish would be best for recipes meant to bring an expansion or increase. Use your imagination to make best use of the dishes you already have.

You have a lot of leeway in selecting the order in which to combine your ingredients. There are some guidelines, however, to help ensure that your magickal food comes out delicious and perfect.

In general, if you're baking, mix all dry ingredients first (with the possible exception of any spices), and then add any liquid ingredients. This is simply a practical step that can reduce clumping, ensuring an even mix and thorough distribution of ingredients. If your recipe calls for egg, add it last if possible, as egg is a magickal binder that can fuse together the energies of your other ingredients. It does the same thing if added in the middle of the recipe, but adding it last does maximize its binding powers to a degree.

As for spices, you can add these in at the start of the cooking process, you can add them as it strikes you as your food cooks, or you can add them all at the very end. Spices are likely to be the most potent ingredients in your recipe, so put them in whenever you feel it's time to add that particular power to the mix.

When you put each ingredient into the recipe, be it flour, spinach, or a dash of salt, do it with intent. As you add each ingredient, think of its energy, its magickal attribute. If it helps along your visualization, imagine the bowl glowing a different color or emitting a different sound as you add each food, or say some affirming words expressing the purpose of each ingredient.

Magickal Mixing

When you mix ingredients together, stir with intent. If you like, use a wand to stir. Use a clockwise stirring motion for attraction magick or to draw positive energies into your food, and use a counterclockwise stirring motion for recipes intended for any sort of unwinding, repelling, or undoing. For dishes with a lunar theme, clockwise stirring relates to the waxing or full moon, while counterclockwise stirring relates to the waning or dark moon.

You can also incorporate the magickal meaning of numbers into the stirring process, counting as you stir in sets of 3, 7, 9, or whatever number seems appropriate for the intent of the food you're preparing. Three is a good number for nearly any magick, as is seven. These numbers are full of magickal power, and they are associated with sacred energies and good luck. Nine is a good number for strength, protection, defense, or any sort of containing or binding action.

Stirring speed is another factor that you can adjust to suit your intent. If your magickal food is intended to slow something down, or if its charm is intended to work gradually over time, stir slowly. If the food is meant to speed up the attainment of a goal, stir fast. Stir at a moderate speed most of the time, with bursts of super speed or super slowness here and there for a boost of power.

You can also trace symbols into the food while you stir, moving your stirring utensil in the shape of a heart, pentacle, dollar sign, rune, or anything else that strikes you.

Preparing to Cook

When you turn on the oven or stove, you might wish to call on the power of the sun, fire, or electricity to be present to cook your food to perfection. When you begin heating the food, visualize the magickal outcome you hope to produce. See yourself rich, loved, happy, safe, whatever the goal is, eating a piece of the food you are currently cooking. You can say out loud some words that state the meal's purpose, such as, "These mashed potatoes will reduce quarrels. Cook true; so will it be!"

Stovetop Magick and Fun in the Oven

If you're cooking on the stovetop, continue thinking of your intent, raising energy, as you periodically stir, flip, or otherwise work with the ingredients as they heat. Raise the energy in the food to a fever pitch just as it is finishing up, and as you turn off the heat, send a final burst of power into the meal.

If you're baking in the oven, affirm your intent as you put the food in to heat, then relax until it's ready. As you take the food out of the oven, in your own words think or say something to affirm the success of your magick. For instance, you might say something like, "This magick food is ready! It will produce a feeling of happiness in all who eat it!"

Eat Up!

You can add a new layer of magick to your finished recipe by topping it with empowered fruit, butter, honey, salt, or pepper. You can even empower the serving utensils if you like, so that they infuse the food with more magickal energy as they move through it. As you eat, think about the food's magickal energy going into your body and filling you with a new vibration, be it a feeling of wealth brought on by a piece of prosperity bread or a feeling of soft sweetness brought on by a slice of romance pizza.

The highest magick of food is in its sustaining, nourishing energy, so whatever specific the food is intended for, also take time to notice the fact that you are nourishing your body and spirit, taking care of yourself by absorbing both nutrients and magickal energy.

Just as you love your friends and family, the earth, and animals, love yourself and see taking care of yourself as a sacred act. You are part of something much bigger, after all, so who are you to neglect the precious and necessary piece of the universal puzzle that is yourself?

Magickal cooking can be very healthy or very unhealthy, depending on the ingredients you use. Whole grain flours are more nutritious than refined flours, and the more you can avoid refined sugar, the better. You can substitute ¾ cup honey for 1 cup of sugar in your recipes, and you can also experiment with date sugar and frozen fruit juices as alternative sweeteners. Unhealthy foods are delicious, too, of course, and eating a little junk food on occasion isn't likely to do much damage. Just do your best to most often make healthy choices in your magickal cooking, and enjoy the feeling of cherishing yourself while you work up some healthy magick.

Magical Attributes of Edible Ingredients

Keep in mind that some ingredients taste awful if used in large quantities. However, you can add a tiny amount of any ingredient to impart its magick to the food without affecting the flavor. Remember also that it is not necessary for every ingredient in your recipe to have a magickal purpose. Using just one or two special ingredients, along with your magickal cooking techniques, will do the trick. Here are a few easy to come by magickal ingredients that can be used to help you achieve your goals while you cook; this is not a definitive list by any means and you should consult an herbal for further reading as you develop your own ideas about other edibles:

Almond: freedom, transformation, movement, wealth, psychic awareness, effective communication, travel, wind magick, intelligence

Apple: love, good luck, happiness, health, dream magick, friendship, calming, bringing rain

Apricot: love, good luck, health

Banana: calming, friendship

Cherry: love, romantic passion, calming, dream magick, health, peace, happiness

Cocoa: strength, energy, love, psychic awareness, passion, happiness, health

Coconut: love, peace, friendship, calming, dream magick

Corn: health, strength, wealth, stability

Egg: binding, polarities, attracting, fertility

Flax: protection, strength, health, good luck

Honey: success, strength, fertility, growth, inspiration, friendship, love, sweetness, dream magick, passion

Maple syrup: love, energy, success, wealth

Milk: binding, fertility, abundance, growth

Mushrooms: spirit communication, dream magick, wisdom

Noodles: longevity, health, good luck

Olives: love, passion, wealth, health

Onion: strength, defense, health

Peach: love, friendship, peace, passion, pleasure, health, calming

Potato: strength, stability, tenacity, health

Rice: health, prosperity

Strawberry: love, happiness, overcoming shyness, good luck, friend-ship

Tomato: love, happiness, friendship, calming

Water: can be empowered for any goal; generally positive; especially useful for purification, inspiration, and love

Magickally Delicious

Any recipe you have can be transformed into a recipe for magickal food. Just add your own rituals and magickal techniques to the cooking process. When using another person's recipe, you can (and should) substitute ingredients or add in extra ingredients to best reflect your spell's intentions. Find ways to make each act of cooking a magickal experience, and you'll add excitement to your food preparation and new inspiration and power to your spellwork.

EXERCISE

1. Do you think food possesses inherent magickal qualities? Do you think certain foods are more potent than others?
2. How could you add magick to these cooking actions?
    Slicing
    Stirring
    Boiling
    Blending
    Kneading
    Open flame grilling

3. What are some different ways to empower magickal food ingredients?

4. How could carrying magickal food with you on the go be useful?

5. What are some ingredients you could use in a magickal recipe to promote good luck?

Taking It Further

What other applications for magickal food can you think up? Do you think it's ethical to give someone magickal food without his or her knowledge? As you experiment with magickal cooking, write down your recipes and note your successes. Research the magickal use of food throughout history to inspire your mystical culinary artistry. Find out about Chinese noodle making, fruit lore, and anything else about food that interests you. Don't let yourself be intimidated by difficult recipes; practice new cooking techniques to improve your skills, and have confidence that your meals will pack a magickal punch. Magickal cooking will strengthen your spellcasting power and versatility, and it is also a great way to continue progressing forward through daily magick practice.

12

Magickal Mistakes and How to Avoid Them

Spell failure can be a disillusioning experience. When we discover magick, it offers such promise, such unlimited potential—we feel inspired and empowered to truly transform our lives in exactly the ways we desire. Then at some point or another we perform a bit of magick that just falls flat. We want to know why, and we want to know how to fix it.

A witch's magick can never be completely lost; when spells aren't working, there's usually a simple reason and an easy remedy. Although magick sometimes proves ineffective for reasons beyond our control, more often than not, spell failure is preventable, the direct consequence of our own actions. From mislaid magick to perpetual spellcasting, many magickal maladies can be avoided once you understand their triggers. Learning to recognize and avoid the pitfalls and mistakes that cause magick to falter will improve your technique and increase the success of your spells, as knowing what not to do will make what you choose to do all the more effective.

Don't let yourself be the cause of these magickal disasters:

Spell Regression

What It Is
Magickal energy associated with a recently cast spell is re-coded, reverting the spell back to an earlier stage and aborting the magickal process.

What Causes It
Dwelling on earlier stages of the magickal process after a spell has been performed re-codes the energy, as it is still associated with you and very easy for you to access, reverting the spell back to whatever part of the ritual you were thinking of. Examples include recounting the details of a currently active spell to a friend, mentally replaying images from the ceremony you performed last week, or emotionally or mentally focusing on the initial need for the spell.

How to Avoid It
Once you've cast a spell, do your best to put the matter and the magick out of your mind. As soon as you finish performing a magickal rite and you've taken a moment to recuperate, immerse yourself in a mentally or emotionally engaging activity. This will put your thoughts off the spell so the magick can progress, preventing failure due to mental interference.

It's important to note that spell regression can occur at any point before the magick achieves its goal. Take steps to combat the problem immediately following spellwork, and also at any time after when you find yourself dwelling on the spell.

Try one of these activities to clear your head after spellwork and avoid spell regression:

- *Organize, rearrange, and de-clutter:* Clear clutter out of a drawer, organize your wardrobe, rearrange the furniture—household tasks that engage you mentally will give you something else to think about other than the protection candles you just anointed or the manifestation incense you just burned. If thoughts of the spell do creep into your head, get right back to your project and think of how just as you are clearing the clutter and rearranging your space more effectively, you are also clearing the way for your spell's continued progress.

- *Fantasize:* Put your mind off your magick by letting it play in the gutter—fantasizing consumes us mentally and emotionally, making dwelling on the just performed spell nearly impossible. Watch a movie starring your favorite sexy celebrity, gaze at a photo of your lover, or imagine the delightful details of a thrilling sexual encounter you'd like to experience. You'll soon be consumed by fantasy, and the ins and outs of spellwork will be the last thing on your mind. Should your fantasy falter and you slip back into thoughts that could cause spell regression, simply direct your sexual energy toward the spell's completion, envisioning success and sending your power to further support that reality's manifestation.

- *Read and write:* Read a book. Write a letter to a friend. Make out a grocery list. Reading and writing require us to focus and pay attention, making it easy to banish thoughts of currently active spells. If thoughts of the spell do manage to drift through your head while you're reading, visualize the magick in its completed stage, entirely successful. Then firmly shut the book, saying, "The spell is cast; I close the book." If you're writing and your mind happens to wander back to your magick, spell regression can be prevented by writing down a sentence affirming your spell's imminent success.

Mislaid Magick

What It Is
Magick functions in a way the spellcaster hadn't intended, leading to unexpected results and unwanted outcomes.

What Causes It
Mislaid magick occurs when the spell method used contradicts the magickal principles on which the magician is seeking to operate. Magick is an adaptable, creative process, but it does tend to function in certain ways and under certain guidelines. Ill-designed spells and sloppy magick can cause energy to be coded in a way that was not intended, in effect casting an entirely different spell with an entirely different magickal result.

How to Avoid It
To prevent mislaid magick, take care when planning and executing your spellwork. Here are some common mistakes to avoid to make sure your magick works just the way you want it to:

- *Mismatched mediums:* A powder absorbed through physical contact will be useless if the subject of your spell lives an ocean away. A talisman crafted to ease tensions at work will be ineffectual locked in a drawer at your home. A spell meant to attract a lover will last longer and work better if the magickal energy is sent out into the world rather than ingested in a potion for a one-time effect. Making sure the medium, or form, of your spell makes sense for the goal you are hoping to achieve will produce better results. For short-lived yet powerful effects, try potions. For magick intended to support a personal transformation or self-improvement goal, talismans and ritual baths work nicely. For spellwork to affect a particular person or place nearby, powders work well. For fast-acting, on-the-spot magick, try a simple word, number, or visualization charm. For far-reaching magickal goals, a full-blown ritual or spell is best. These suggestions need not be strictly adhered to, of course. As long as the medium is not in opposition or contradiction to the goal, it will work.

- *Sloppy spellwork:* Spilled potions and powders, dirty wands, mildewed herbs, soured anointing oils—these are just a few of the messy problems that can lead to mislaid magick. Old ingredients that have spoiled or gone stale can do the same to your magick, ruining spells and causing them to function in ways contrary to your wishes. Use moldy herbs in a sachet meant to attract a lover, and you might attract the romantic attentions of an unsavory character. Put old, stale herbs in the blend, and your magickally manifested love affair might be devoid of passion. Spill a banishing powder on your dog's bed, and you might have to find yourself a new pet. Forget to clean the attraction potion off your wand and use it for defensive magick, and the threat of danger might be drawn to you that much closer. Fortunately, a little neatness and care is all that's needed to stave off mislaid magick caused by sloppy spellwork. Take care to seal up potions and powders immediately after use, and label your ingredients so you'll know exactly what each is and how old it is. Clean your ritual tools before or after each use, paying special attention to anything used in dark, defensive, or banishing magick.

- *Faulty planning:* Mislaid magick also occurs when a spell goal does not fit with the actual needs of the practitioner. For example, casting a spell to land a new job when the real issue at hand is beating an old addiction is not likely to be effective. Likewise, a mother neglecting her parenting duties will probably not succeed in magickally attracting a wild and dangerous lover. Think out your magick and make sure your goal is something you are truly ready for, something that makes sense in your life for where you are right now. Sometimes we simply have not taken the preliminary steps to prepare us for what our spells might bring, and as a result, the magick refuses to do its trick, or does another sort of trick instead. Plan your spells in accordance with your actual needs, and you will avoid mislaid magick caused by faulty planning.

Perpetual Spellcasting

What It Is

Magick is spontaneously performed through everyday actions and thoughts without the practitioner's knowledge, potentially counteracting previous spells and creating chaos. Signs of perpetual spellcasting may include lingering feelings of disorientation, unexplainable excitability or anxiety, and feelings of being drained or fatigued.

What Causes It

The spellcaster unintentionally remains in a state of ritual consciousness following a magickal working, resulting in what amounts to the Midas touch of magick. While performing a rite of magick, we're in a mental state in which we code energy through our consciousness, will, and intent. If you fail to disconnect or "turn off" your ritual consciousness after an act of magick, you might become an unknowing vehicle for perpetual spellcasting, your every movement and every imagining coding the energies surrounding you without the benefit of your awareness.

How to Avoid It

Grounding yourself after every magickal working prevents perpetual spellcasting. Through the process of grounding, your energies are consciously detached from the rite just performed and your mind returns to its normal, non-magickal "resting" state. We have the ability to slip easily between ritual consciousness and everyday "regular" consciousness, but with this skill comes the responsibility to do so intentionally. We turn it on and we turn it off. We do our best to control it. Grounding after rituals is a way to exercise such control. Without it, we risk acting as perpetrators of accidental magick, which too often results in magickal accidents. There are many grounding techniques, and it's helpful to try different methods. Here are some quick and effective ways to ground after magick and prevent perpetual spellcasting from wreaking havoc and impeding success:

- *Wash it off:* Water has a cleansing and soothing effect on the psyche, making it a perfect ingredient to use for grounding. After spellwork, take a bath or shower to calm your nerves and turn off the magickal mental process. As it grounds you, the water washes away any lingering traces of ritual consciousness so that you won't accidentally undo your own spells by perpetually casting new ones.

- *Ground with the ground:* It's called "grounding" for a reason. One way to ground yourself after a ritual is to simply touch the ground. The earth brims with a stabilizing force that centers and tempers energies, and touching the bare ground brings a clear end to spellwork and sets your consciousness back to its everyday duties. Lay down on the ground or kneel and place both palms flat against the dirt. Feel the earth energy course through your body, pulling you toward it and bringing you into harmony with its vibration. As you ground with the ground, your mind is readjusted from a magickal state into a more mundane and less volatile state, thus preventing perpetual spellcasting from dashing your magickal dreams.

- *Shake it off:* The body and mind are connected, and vigorous physical movement is an easy and fast way to ground yourself after magick. Shake your hands and arms, your feet and legs. Dance around. Do a few push-ups or jumping jacks. The motion of your body will pull your mind out of ritual consciousness and ground you to a more mundane mental state, ensuring that any magick you perform will be the result of intention rather than the side effect of perpetual spellcasting.

Magickal Fallout

What It Is

Magickal fallout is the unintended and unfortunate karmic effect of magick that doesn't play by your rules.

What Causes It

Attempting too often to bypass your own rules, ignore the limits, or break the taboos of magick can lead to magickal fallout. Examples include a curse backfiring on the caster, a prosperity spell bringing a sudden expense, or a love spell attracting the very person you hope to repel. Magickal fallout is caused when the actions, intent, or emotions of the spellcaster violate fundamental magickal constants or ethics, leading to karmic consequences.

How to Avoid It

Know the limits, rules, and taboos of magick, and don't attempt to break them without first putting some serious thought into the matter. Ethics are somewhat subjective, and there are no strict and structured laws when it comes to magick; what is most important is that your magick not violate your own personal standards and beliefs. Consider these points to develop your own ethical guidelines to keep your good karma intact and avoid magickal fallout:

- *Karma:* Karma is your best friend and worst enemy. A popular adage adhered to in magick, the law of karma states that whatever energies you send out are returned to you, often in a threefold manner. Lay just one little curse on someone undeserving, and three stints of terrible misfortune will likely befall you. There is a time for cursing, but it's not very often. In certain extreme circumstances, for instance, when there is a real threat of serious danger, "bad" magick can be performed without garnering too much negative karma. However, even when negative magick is justified, it does have consequences on the spellcaster. To perform very dark magick, the practitioner must raise and release very dark energies, and this action does produce some karmic effects. If the spell is really necessary, these effects are usually mild. If, on the other hand, the spellcaster is not in any real danger and is merely being mean or wanting revenge, casting a dark spell will have lasting, unfortunate karmic results. You must carefully weigh the risks and benefits and decide for yourself on a case-by-case basis whether or not casting a curse is wise, worth it, and justified.

- *Limits and love spells:* Magick has its limits; one such line is drawn at love spells. While it's perfectly acceptable and effective to cast a general love spell to attract more love to your life, casting a love spell on a specific person will not work properly. It's quite possible to magickally cause a specific person to become obsessed or infatuated, but it is not at all possible to magickally create actual love. Love spells geared at specific people "work" in the sense that the person might indeed become taken with you, but the feeling will not run deep and it will fade fast. Control and manipulation are not ways to express love, and a relationship based on these factors is bound to disappoint and cause misery. However deep the desire, casting a spell to make Dan the Postman fall madly in love with you is simply not possible. So what about making other people fall in love? Does it work if the spell is not for you, but is aiming instead to get Dick and Jane together? The answer is no, it doesn't work, unless of course Dick and Jane are already digging on each other, in which case the spell would simply remove any barriers in the way of their love affair. If, however, Dick is madly in love with Sue, casting a spell to make him fall in love with Jane will only make him fall that much harder for Sue. It's just the way it works. To avoid the consequences of magickal fallout, play by the rules and direct your love spells to a general, non-specific audience of potential lovers.

- *Taboos:* There are a few magickal actions that should generally not be done, as they can cause serious magickal fallout. There are two breakable taboos and one unbreakable taboo. Break the breakables only very rarely, or only when doing so is truly necessary. Here they are; you've been warned:

1. *Don't intentionally hurt animals or people!* Unbreakable taboo. Directly or indirectly physically harming people or animals in the course of performing magick will call a flood of magickal fallout. Cruelty is the last thing you want karma to return to you. Magicians who are hateful and seek to hurt, injuring animals to use in spells, taking sexual advantage of vulnerable covenmates, etc., will quickly lose any real power. Their spells are doomed to fail, just as they doom their own souls with each

hurtful action. Even in cases where a curse is called for, the magick should not be focused on causing physical harm.

2. *Don't play around!* Breakable taboo. Avoid performing exclusively frivolous, unnecessary, manipulative magick just for fun. Doing so will reveal your own shallowness and selfishness, setting loose a lot of chaotic magickal fallout and thwarting any real spiritual progress. Magicians who want to increase their power and truly know the magickal arts must take their practice seriously and not cast serious spells lightly. It's okay every now and then to cast a frivolous spell just for fun, but save the practice for rare occasions. Similarly, it's perfectly fine to use unnecessary spellwork to help develop your magickal skills and for experiment's sake, as long as the spells you're doing aren't harmful. But if this is the only type of magick being cast and more serious and sacred spellwork is being ignored, the witch's spirituality and magickal power will suffer. It's the overall picture that matters. Deciding on a whim to try to make it snow, for instance, isn't likely to cause magickal fallout if it's been a while since you've done such a spell. On the other hand, if you've been magickally controlling the weather for a solid month without good reason, you'll soon see a heavy rainfall of unpleasant consequences. Avoid magickal fallout by generally holding to the "Don't play around" taboo, breaking it only rarely.

3. *Don't brag or show off!* Breakable taboo. So you cast a spell, and it worked impeccably. You're feeling proud, and you want to boast about your powers to the whole world. Don't. Tell your best friend some minimal details if you must. Tell your dog. But don't go shouting about it in order to impress or gain dominance. Magickal prowess is a personal pride. We can't help but feel giddy and pleased with ourselves when our magick goes right, but we're humbled knowing that the success of a spell was by no means "all us." Ultimately, magick is a prayer, a question, a way to politely ask for a favor. We control it no more than a clock "controls" time. We can certainly become

experts in the art of making such requests. We can definitely get more magickal power and improve our ability to use it to its full potential. We can be magickal masters—but we are never masters of magick. We don't boss it around; it's not a slave to our wishes. Prevent magickal fallout by keeping boasting to a minimum. And whenever you do feel a little too pleased with yourself, you can put your ego in check by humbly repeating in whispered words your magickal request.

Mistakes Averted, Danger Thwarted

Now that you know the most common mistakes that cause spells to fail, you can do your best to avoid them. And if a bit of magick does go awry, you'll be better able to pinpoint the problem and you'll be more likely to avoid making the same mistake twice.

Exercise

1. Have you ever broken a taboo or rule of magick? What were the consequences?
2. What has been your most successful spell to date?
3. What spells have you tried that failed? Do you have a better idea now of why the magick didn't work?
4. Identify trouble spots that could cause a magickal mishap in the following scenarios:

• You work a spell to make the hot cashier at the gardening store you frequent ask you out on a date.

• You're on the verge of losing your home, and you work a charm to bring more excitement into your life.

• After performing a protective spell, you call your mother and tell her about the threat and your fear.

• Your body is still tingling after the banishing ritual you just performed, and you decide it's the right time to cut your hair.

Taking It Further

What other causes of spell failure can you think of? Keep a written or mental spell journal and note both the positive and negative results of your magick. When a spell falls short, examine your recent thought processes and actions to see if you can discover exactly what caused the magick to fail. Could you have done anything to prevent the magickal mistake? If so, what? Likewise, when a spell works phenomenally well, explore the choices you made that helped ensure success. Understanding what helps and what hinders the magickal process for you personally will enable you to manipulate energy more efficiently and effectively.

13

Rules to Break

Alittle rebellion now and then keeps us vibrant. After all, we don't want the magickal arts to end up all homogenized in unquestioning conformity, although the way some of us act, you'd think that's just what we're going for! "That's wrong," "You can't do that," "It's unethical"—these are phrases unfortunately heard in mainstream Christian churches and underground Pagan circles alike. Most of us think for ourselves and are turned off by such judgmental antics. We don't accept things at face value—we question and investigate. But it's sometimes difficult to stand up in the face of conventional wisdom and declare yourself in dissent: "Evil" is something we might expect to be called once in a blue moon by an ignorant outsider, not by our own fellow witches, though it certainly happens! Be that as it may, it is time for our magickal practices to evolve beyond the limits suggested by another person's moral compass or belief system! Consider alternative perspectives on traditional regulations and restrictions of magick (including those described in the previous chapter), and decide for yourself whether or not to play by the rules.

Magickally Affecting Others

Many practitioners of the magickal arts are adamant about never doing magick to affect other people without the other person's knowledge or consent. It is widely believed that doing so is unethical due to the fact that it interferes with the other person's free will. But is doing magick to affect others *always* unethical, given the pressing need in our society to relieve suffering and overcome the hateful, violent forces that strive to mess it up for the rest of us? Is it possible this rule has expired? Perhaps the rule has been generally misinterpreted and misunderstood over the years.

Taking a closer look, we find that, really, we interfere with other people's free will all the time, and with good reason. If you see a kid about to run into the road, for example, wouldn't grabbing the kid and holding him back be the right thing to do, even though you're technically interfering with the child's free will? Likewise, locking your door at night or performing a spell to ward off thieves might interfere with a burglar's free will to rob you. If someone were about to jump your little brother, wouldn't you do your best to gain control over the attacker, in order to prevent that attacker from exerting their free will to beat somebody up? How about if a friend were about to drive drunk—wouldn't it be permissible to take the keys, thereby tampering with your friend's free will to risk lives? How would doing a spell to prevent a suicidal acquaintance from buying a gun be any different?

If it's accepted that it's sometimes okay to interfere with another person's free will using non-magickal techniques, then the only reason for believing that magickally affecting another's free will is inherently bad is if you believe that magick itself is inherently bad. Seeing as you're reading this book, I'm guessing you don't feel that way!

If you're following this logic, you know you can trust in your own ability to be sensible when it comes to using such magick. Just as it's okay to walk a dog on a leash but not okay to keep a dog trapped in a cage, the ethics of magickally affecting other people are unique for each situation and are largely dependent on what is needed and necessary in a particular circumstance. For instance, there would typically be no reason to work a spell to make your best friend wake up suddenly in the middle of the night, just as there would typically be no reason to trap a dog in a cage. In either situation, it would be an unethical constriction of another creature's free will. But just as a dog with rabies *should* be put in a cage, if you had a strong psychic sensation in the middle of the night that your friend's house was on fire, and she doesn't answer your phone call, then doing a spell to wake her up would be perfectly helpful.

Trust that you are a good person who has the ability to discern what is needed in a particular situation, and use your best judgment. Those powers weren't meant to be hoarded only for your own self; you've got to put them to good use to help other people!

The Case for Cursing

Most magickal practitioners avoid so-called black magick, or cursing, at all costs. It's seen as unethical, an abuse of power that is downright wrong. In most cases, the axiom "harm none" rings true, but as is the nature of existence, there are always exceptions.

We live in extreme times, in a world fraught with needless violence and the cruelty of war. The time of oppressive regimes and power-hungry warmongers has passed, or rather, it should be passed. We must take on and thwart these destructive and baneful forces with an equally powerful resistance. Fluffy bunnies don't win battles. We can't overcome the evils of the world with smiles and hugs alone. We must use our power—all our power—in order to conquer that which must be conquered for the greater good of humanity and life on earth.

Nature destroys as well as sustains, and we too have roles to play on both sides of the fence. We must protect, yes. We must heal, certainly. Undoubtedly, we must manifest positive vibrations in our efforts to help each other and our planet. But it takes more than good vibes to undo the channels that seek to bind enlightenment. We must use all weapons necessary. We must bite back, we must curse, we must hex, we must bind and contain these negative forces with all the might we can muster.

But what about karma? Isn't there a price to pay for negative acts of magick? Certainly, there's a price, and pay it we must, but with a little foresight and planning, that price can be greatly reduced. Say you're working a spell to create peace between two warring nations. You might bind their weapons, thwart their leaders, or take other similar measures. To keep karma at bay, you would simply take the law of reciprocation into your own hands, casting the spell to take effect in your own life as well as affecting the warring parties. Are you quarreling with your lover? Do you have a habit of shooting out criticisms like a stream of bullets? Keep these things in mind as you cast your magick, and the karmic effect of laying a curse will have a positive impact on your personal sphere.

Time and How to Conquer It

Timing magickal acts in accord with astral, lunar, and seasonal energies can indeed add power and effectiveness to your spellwork. If the moon phase and current season happen to be perfectly auspicious for the spell you're casting, then there's no problem. Often, though, the need for magick is urgent. We can't always wait for the moon to wane; we don't always have the luxury of waiting around for spring. However, as time is cyclical, it's possible to access the energies of any season, any hour, any lunar conditions or planetary positions, at any time whatsoever. You can reap the benefits of magickal timing regardless of where the moon and the wheel of the year are in their cycles.

If you know the best times for working various acts of magick, you can learn to invoke the energies of those times no matter what the clock and the calendar indicate. The key is to create the conditions you seek, using symbols, tarot cards, art, colors, and herbs to manifest the energetic vibrations of the lunar phase or season most appropriate to your particular magickal working. Gather as many items as possible to help you tune in to the appropriate time frame, place these objects on your altar or around your ritual area, and have at it.

Here are some guidelines for optimally timing your magick; use the symbols and colors listed to help you mimic and invoke any season or lunar phase any day of the year. Take another look at magickal timing, bypass conventional wisdom, and learn to make your spells run like clockwork anytime:

Lunar Phases

Waning moon (full moon to dark moon): A good time for introspection, absorbing magickal knowledge, spells designed to diminish or expel negative energies, self-improvement magick, summoning hidden inner strength, exploring grief and rebirth, transformation, banishing obstacles and illness, and expressing gratitude. The night of the dark moon is particularly favorable for divination, dream magick, and communication with the spirit realm.

- *Symbols:* the Moon tarot card in the reversed (upside-down) position, a dark-surfaced scrying glass, a solid black circle, a drawing or photo of a dark or waning moon
- *Colors:* black, dark gray, or purple
- *Herbs:* poppy seeds, dried lemon

Waxing moon (dark moon to full moon): A good time for outward expression, spells designed to increase or attract positive energies, putting magickal knowledge into practice, magick intended to improve the world or the community, embarking on new adventures, creating and seizing opportunity, and bringing love and romance. The night of the full moon is well suited for rituals of exaltation and reverence, and is also the time in the lunar cycle when magickal energy is at its height.

- *Symbols:* the Moon or High Priestess tarot card in the upright position, silver coins, a drawing or photo of the full or waxing moon
- *Colors:* white, red, or silver
- *Herbs:* lemon, coconut

Seasonal Cycles

Winter: A time of contemplation, lunar energies, the home, hope, tenacity, introspection and retrospection, communicating with the dead, and inner transformation.

- *Symbols:* the Hermit tarot card, ice, drawings or photos of winter scenes
- *Colors:* white, dark gray, or black
- *Herbs:* holly, pine, and other evergreens

Spring: A time of growth, new beginnings, sowing seeds, creativity, romance, union, fertility, and both physical and emotional renewal.

- *Symbols:* the High Priestess or World tarot card, real or artificial flowers, drawings or photos of spring scenes
- *Colors:* light green, pastel colors
- *Herbs:* flowers of all types, dill

Summer: A time of fruition and maturation, solar energies, action, strength, and vigor.

- *Symbols:* the Sun or Empress tarot card in the upright position, citrine or turquoise stones, drawings or photos of summer scenes
- *Colors:* green or bright yellow
- *Herbs:* dandelion, sunflowers, oranges

Autumn: A time of gathering, preparation, showing gratitude, reaping what was sown, outward change, and shedding away the old.

- Symbols: The Emperor or Death tarot card in the upright position, real or artificial fall foliage, drawings or photos of fall scenes

- Colors: orange, golden yellow, brown, red
- Herbs: moss, apples, squash, nuts

<u>EXERCISE</u>

1. Can you think of a situation in which interfering with another person's free will would be a good idea? If so, would you be willing to use magick in the situation?
2. If a known rapist were stalking your daughter, in addition to taking legal action, would you also curse them?
3. Is it okay to use magick to affect others as long as the magick is intended to have a positive effect?
4. Is it okay to use such magick if the intent is negative, as long as it is justified by the situation?
5. Does time always matter in magick? Why or why not?
6. What are some of the traditional rules of magick you disagree with? Do you have additional rules of your own?

Taking It Further

As a thoughtful, spiritually evolving magickal being, it's not just your right, but your duty to decide for yourself the ethical standards by which you abide. Think about your morals when it comes to magick, and make your own list of rules and exceptions. Doing so is yet another way to personalize your spellcraft, and when you make it your own and you're not afraid to push the boundaries, magick can truly work wonders.

14

Better Magickal Goal Setting

Spell goals are the motivation behind your magick. If those goals are ill-designed or anything less than spectacular, your magick is not likely to meet its mark. Simply put, better, more effective goal setting leads to better, more powerful magick. Here's how to do it.

Specific but Flexible

You'll achieve better results and be able to more accurately evaluate the effectiveness of your magick by choosing specific rather than vague goals for your spellwork. For example, say you cast a spell for general prosperity. The next day, a neighbor might come by to give you a bushel of tomatoes from her garden. A week later, you get a small promotion at your job. A month later, you find a ten dollar bill on the sidewalk. Which of these situations was a direct result of the spell? Was it old fashioned neighborly love or magick that manifested the tomatoes? Was it hard work and assertiveness alone that landed you the promotion, or did your spell help create the circumstances that made that opportunity arise when it did? Was it merely a coincidence that you found ten dollars on the ground, or was this a gift direct from the gods? When your spell goals are vague and too broad, it's impossible to separate the results of the magick from happenstance.

Further, when spell goals are too general, the effects of your magick will be spread out and diluted rather than focused and concentrated. You can achieve greater effects and better evaluate the success of your spells by setting specific, targeted goals for each magickal working.

Let's take another look at the above example, this time setting a more focused goal. Say you've worked a spell to get a substantial pay raise. In this case, every bit of energy you put into the spell will focus on bringing you that raise. The magickal power will not be spread thin, nor will it be diluted or dissipated. The magick will be targeted and concentrated on manifesting your specific goal, and it therefore has a greater chance of being effective. Now say your neighbor brings over those tomatoes, say you find that ten dollar bill on the sidewalk. Since you worked a specific spell targeted to bring you a raise, you won't mistake the tomatoes or the ten dollars for spell results; you'll know your spell is still active until you get that raise, and when you get it, you'll know your spell has worked.

But suppose you don't get the raise for whatever reason, but you do buy a lottery ticket and win fifty dollars. If you've worked a focused spell to bring you a raise and you don't get it, you'll know that particular spell failed, regardless of your winning lottery ticket, and you'll know to adjust your goal or your method to produce the magickal results you desire. If you worked a general, unfocused prosperity spell and the same occurred—no raise but a winning lottery ticket—you wouldn't really know if your spell had succeeded or failed, so you wouldn't be able to ascertain how to make future spells more effective. Being specific not only helps spells succeed, but also helps you troubleshoot what went wrong when they don't succeed.

Specific does not mean rigid, however. Flexibility is just as important as focus. Taking a look at our example again, let's examine what can happen when our goals are too rigid. Suppose you've set a focused goal to manifest that raise at work, setting the goal even more specifically to manifest exactly two hundred dollars a month added to your paycheck. Such a spell may indeed manifest a two hundred dollar raise, but the rigidity of the goal might prevent an even greater manifestation of your desires. Perhaps your boss had been planning on giving you an extra three hundred dollars each month; perhaps that boss was also contemplating giving you a company car, or offering greater health insurance benefits at a lower cost. The rigid parameters of your spell's goal would set these occurrences outside the boundaries of possibilities and might prevent them from coming to pass.

Magick doesn't make assumptions. It does what we tell it to do. We as spellcasters cannot foresee all the possible results of a spell, and through our own limited thinking, we may inadvertently limit our own success. This is why it is wise to build in to your spells a flexibility clause. A flexibility clause may be something as simple as a statement requesting that the magick manifest itself "in the greatest way possible" or "in the most beneficial manner."

Further, when visualizing your goal as you work a spell, see yourself having attained the goal, but avoid visualizing exactly how that goal will be attained. For instance, considering our example once more, you might visualize depositing a larger paycheck in the bank, or see clearly your wallet overflowing with cash. But you would avoid visualizing specific dollar amounts, and you would refrain from imagining the exact words your boss might use to tell you about the raise. Magick needs focus, but it is ultimately a creative force, and creativity requires flexibility in order to reach its full potential. Just as you might commission an artist to paint a picture of a tree, you should give your spells specific directions. But you would not demand the artist use only certain colors or only certain paintbrushes to create that tree, and just the same, you would not tell your magick the exact method through which to achieve its function.

Fortune Favors the Bold

Magickal goals should be bold and daring, not shy and uncertain! When our goals aren't good enough, there's simply not enough gold at the end of the rainbow to make us work to get there. On the other hand, if what we want to achieve is so glorious, so crystal clear we just have to get it, we strive with all our might and put the full force of our magickal power of love and consciousness into getting us there. When our goals have purpose, a message to convey, a mending to render on the threads of existence, the flow of magickal power that comes rushing to help us is mighty indeed.

It's important to know your overall goals as a player in this great act we call magick. What, ultimately, are you hoping that magick can do for you? Are you willing to take this work on in a greater extent, to the benefit of reality at large? Your ultimate magickal goals will grow and be refined as you progress along your path, but it helps to have a sense of what your main magickal mission is at the moment. We witches can choose to work random spells randomly at the dictates and whims of current reality, or we can choose what we will do with our magick and do it in a big, bold way. We grow spiritually and psychically when we really go for it magickally, and the thing we grow into is greater magickal power.

So use your magick boldly and proudly, setting far-reaching goals with lasting positive effects. With love in your heart and a brain in your head, trust in your own power to see and sense what must be done. It's fine to do magick for the little things too, of course, but the witch who *only* uses magick in small ways misses out on a deep pool of magickal power just waiting to be called into action.

Putting It into "Words"

As a succinct summary of the spell as a whole, an articulated spell goal is concentrated magick, and it can pack a punch if properly delivered. Putting spell goals into words doesn't have to be a tricky and tongue-tying endeavor; in fact, spell goals need not be articulated through spoken, signed, or written language at all. You can express your spell goals mentally or through other means of communication such as symbolism or movement.

Articulating spell goals in a straightforward, concise, and purposeful manner ensures your message will be received and understood. Don't incorporate any unnecessary or less than totally honest information in your spell goal. Get right to the point and be precise and genuine about exactly what you're going for, communicating your spell goal in the simplest form possible. For example, don't use fifty words when five will do, or create a complex, multi-layered sigil to convey your goal when a simpler symbol would say it all.

Also be sure to articulate spell goals in a way that serves the purpose of the communication. What exactly are you trying to tell the magickal energies you're working with? Make sure your instructions are complete and relevant. For example, suppose you get a call that your friend's car broke down and they're stranded on the highway. You've phoned AAA, but you also decide to work magick to help get the car going again. You don't need to articulate in your spell goal anything about your friend's need for a *new* car, no matter how true that might be. You simply want to get the current car started right now, and that's what the magickal forces you're calling on to help you need to know. Well, that, and a good idea of about where the car is located.

Another aspect of articulating spell goals to suit their purpose is considering your audience. Exactly what energies are you using in this particular working? How do these energies best receive information, and in what ways can you communicate with these forces? For example, a musical witch who was working a spell with Pan might best convey her spell's goal to her deity by playing a short song on a flute, sending the music off through the air. Keep in mind your audience (the forces and energies you're communicating with in magick) as well as the reason for the communication, and you'll be able to skillfully articulate your spell goal in a way that effectively serves its purpose.

Better Goals, Better Magick

By refining our magickal goal-setting techniques, we improve the quality of our magick. Be bold, be flexibly specific, stick to the purpose, and get to the point. That's all there is to it. Now actually *choosing* said goals, that's another story, but it's a job that's your own and it's a job you must do. Our magickal goals are a direct expression of our intent, which is a direct reflection of our spirituality. The more we grow spiritually and psychically, the better and bigger are the goals we can envision, and the more precise, potent, and powerful becomes our magick.

EXERCISE

See if you can spot the trouble with the following spell goals. Rewrite them to be more effective.

1. I want more love in my life.
2. I want to get that kind of crappy job I kind of want.
3. I want to be rich.
4. I want to sell my car for $3000.
5. I want to get married, one day, after college and if I meet the right person, that is, I think I'll go to college, maybe not, I want a big wedding, though, so wedding, manifest!
6. I want to travel.
7. I want Bob's job.
8. I want to meet a new lover.
9. I want to show five paintings in the Maple Street Gallery this April.

Taking It Further

What other requirements for good magickal goal setting can you think of? Are there other magickal goal-setting techniques you would like to investigate? Are there other ways of articulating spell goals you've never before tried? Studying magickal rhythm and rhyme, and learning a visual language such as American Sign Language, are great ways to get ideas that will add beauty and variety to your spell goal articulation. What else do you want to know about magickal goals? How can you find out? Right now, think of three magickal goals you would like to achieve. Make them bold, brave, and beautiful, like your own magickal power itself.

15

Better Tools, New Tricks

Magickal tools are just that: tools. They are for us to design and use to help us carry out our jobs as spellworkers, and the more personalized and versatile those tools are, the more ways we can find to build our own road onward. Although not of vital necessity, magickal tools can certainly enhance the effects of spellwork and make it easier to perform. We witches are hands-on types, and many of us find that using tools enriches our practice, giving us an outward tangible medium through which we can express the magick that's going on internally.

Chances are you already have a selection of tools you enjoy using for your magick, but perhaps you've gotten a little bored with your toys and you sometimes just skip them altogether and do your magick solely mentally. Magick works just fine like that, of course, but without the physical ritual that magickal tools can provide, it's very easy to lose focus on the spell at hand. Discover new ways to use tools you already have, and learn how to customize tools in ways you might not have tried before; it's a great way to recharge your practice and revamp your magickal bag of tricks.

Altars

Many magickal people enjoy the process of setting up an altar, transforming a small table, tree stump, or other platform into a special place to cast magick, a place that builds up an energetic charge that strengthens magickal power and enhances psychic abilities. Not all of us have the luxury of setting up a permanent place for spellwork, however. If that's your situation, try making a custom-designed portable altar. Choose a large square of fabric to use like a hobo sack, holding other altar items tied within it. You might use fabric in your favorite color, or make your own mini-quilt with pieces of old ritual clothing that are already infused with your personal magick power. When it's time to work magick, just untie the fabric and spread it out like your very own ready-made table-top.

As your altar naturally builds up a strong magickal charge, you can use it as a magickal slow cooker of sorts. Weekly or monthly, write down on a slip of paper a goal or wish. Then simply place this on your altar, no ceremony required, and see what happens. The altar will often do the spellwork for you.

Your altar also provides a great place to recharge during a frustrating day. When things get hectic, sneak away to your altar for a moment. Let the magickal power of the place pour into you, calming you and giving you strength and control.

Cauldrons

Traditional cauldrons are large cast iron pots with three short legs on the bottom, signifying the three aspects of the female lunar deity, a.k.a. the Triple Moon Goddess. Cauldrons like this are hard to find, but the resourceful and creative witch knows how to use what's on hand! A regular cooking pot or any other fireproof vessel will work perfectly fine. (Copper and aluminum should be avoided, though, as these metals can alter energetic vibrations of plant ingredients.)

Try choosing your makeshift cauldron container based on its materials. Are you more of a modern, easy-going stainless steel type, or are you more old-fashioned and grounded like iron? Are you transparent, wearing your heart on your sleeve? Perhaps a glass pot would suit you best.

To put the cauldron in tune with your unique essence and personality, anoint the inside with a bit of your own energy by rubbing it thoroughly. Increase your cauldron's power further by decorating it with symbols or images that speak to you, engraving the glyphs into the cauldron's surface or painting them on with a waterproof, nonflammable paint. Not just for potion-making, the cauldron is an excellent time-saving tool, as it can be employed to quickly empower magickal ingredients placed inside. You can also use it to purify and recharge many magickal tools at once; just place the tools inside the cauldron for a few hours at the time of the new moon.

You can also try using your cauldron for stress relief. When you're feeling sad or anxious, pour these energies into the cauldron, letting the goddess therein symbolized carry away your woes.

Knives, Mortars, and Pestles

Knives, mortars, and pestles are used to prepare herbal ingredients for magick and to direct energy during spellwork. Functional and flexible, they are highly useful tools for the practical and imaginative witch.

A magickal knife can be used in place of a wand, and is in fact preferable for charms and spells intended to symbolically slash through negative energy. It can also be used to prepare a special offering to the spirits or deities you honor: use the knife to cut off a lock of your own hair to leave as a very personal gift that conveys trust and sacrifice. A magickal knife can be used in the kitchen, too; charm the knife to cut your appetite or to invoke happiness, and use it to slice food.

Although crafting a magickal knife from scratch is out of reach for most witches, it's easy to give a ready-made knife more style and power. Try drawing meaningful symbols on the hilt, or tie around it a piece of your own hair. You might also anoint it with a special oil, tracing the letters of your name onto the blade.

A mortar and pestle provide a magickal way to keep hands strong and flexible; grinding rosemary while you sit is a great exercise for people who suffer from hand cramps or arthritis, as it strengthens the muscles while releasing a soothing, healing energy from the herbs. The mortar and pestle are also useful for curse-breaking magick, stress relief, and freeing trapped energies such as hidden creativity. Simply empower some herbs to represent the energies you're working with, i.e., a curse, stress, or blocked energy, and then grind that up to free these energies and break through bonds to get things moving again. Although mortars and pestles are sold as sets, it's best to find the mortar yourself, such as a rock you find especially appealing or one that has specific attributes you feel would be beneficial.

Candles

Candles are employed in magickal ritual to provide a mystical ambiance, to amplify energy, or to serve as the focal point of a spell.

Candle wax can be used magickally in many ways, from creating wax effigies for use in imitative and image magick, to dripping it in the shapes of signs and symbols to enhance a ritual. Amongst Polish Pagans is a method of candle fortune-telling that involves dripping wax into a glass of water and reading the solidified shapes that form.

Candles can also be used for fire scrying. Simply put yourself into a trance by gazing into the flame and welcome whatever visions come.

Candles can help you build a trusting and friendly relationship with nature, too. Turning off the artificial lights for an hour or two and letting candles illuminate your room instead conserves the earth's resources and also helps you unwind.

For a very unusual experience, try using candles to help you connect with the insect mind. Many bugs are drawn to light, and lighting a candle outside at night will often draw these creatures near you. Put the candle in a glass container so as not to incinerate your new friends, however. Stretch out your consciousness and try to access the mind of the insect kingdom.

Although dangerous and a good way to get hurt if you're not careful, using a candle flame to seal a magickal oath or bond with another person can be an interesting experience of trust and commitment that invokes a powerful shared magick. If you're not comfortable with snuffing out candle flames with your fingers, don't try this. Begin by saying what needs to be said between you and the other person, and take care of any preliminary rituals you might want to incorporate. When the time comes, seal the oath by extinguishing the candle flame between your hands, each person on one side of the candle and bringing the palms together quickly and simultaneously upon the flame.

Try customizing your candle magick by formulating your own system of color attributions. You might also choose a symbol to act as your energetic signature and scratch this into the bottom of every candle. This acts like a calling card you use to tell the powers, "This spell is from me!"

You can also impart your personality when choosing which candles to buy. Do you feel that fancy candles made of exquisite beeswax have the most magickal potential, or are you the sort of person who buys what's cheapest and makes it work? Are paraffin candles best for certain types of magick, and should candles made with synthetics be avoided? Decide what's important and go with what works for you.

If you have kids at home, then you most likely have a perpetual supply of broken crayons on hand. Try melting these down, pour the wax into empty milk cartons or something similar, put in a wick, and make your very own line of recycled candles. The candles will be full of magickal kid power and creative energy that can be useful in a variety of spells.

Crystals and Other Rocks

Like every natural substance, crystals and other rocks have intrinsic magickal power. Each has a distinct vibration, and some rocks, such as crystals, can take on and amplify the energies imparted to them.

Stones are handy; they can serve as very inconspicuous spell containers that can be placed virtually anywhere without notice. Simply release the energy of your spell into the rock, then subtly drop it or hide it in the place where it's meant to activate.

Another use of stones is making music to enhance the ritual experience; tap two rocks together to create a rhythm, or drum on a larger rock with a stick to make your beats. For a long-term spell to remove obstacles, empower a stone with your purpose and place it in a stream to erode away any barriers to your success.

You can also use rocks and crystals to help tell the story of your spell. For instance, if you are working a spell to increase your intuition, you could place a moonstone (associated with psychic powers) on your altar as you utter, "The powers of the moon in all her aspects grant me intuition." You could then place a crystal (which magnifies energy) as you say, "My intuition will be amplified with great power."

Stones are also great stress relievers. Hold a negativity-absorbing hematite or jet stone in your hand and pour into it all your stressful energy. Then grab a citrine or other crystal, letting it flood you with positive magickal power to soothe your soul.

Rocks and crystals can also be empowered and carried with you to attract desired vibrations, placed on affected body parts during healing magic, used similarly to runes for divination, or powdered and used as ingredients in non-drinkable potions and other magickal recipes.

When custom-designing your rock magick, remember that stones can be thrown and also buried or sunk; use this symbolism when crafting spells to banish or delay. Try to find magickal rocks yourself rather than seeking out a lapidary, and when possible, select stones that are in tune with your personal energies and astrological sign.

Magickal Plants

Essential ingredients for many potions, oils, powders, ointments, and incense, magickal plants are incorporated into a wide variety of spells and charms. Although the properties and associations of plants commonly used in magick are well established in various traditions, you should feel free to formulate your own ideas of each plant's magickal aspects. Forget what you know about conventional herbology and really get in touch with the plant's energies right there in the present moment. Explore magickal plants with all your senses and write down your observations.

When selecting plants for magick, play to your strengths, keeping astrological and elemental affinities in mind and choosing plants in tune with your unique vibrations.

It's also a good idea to harmonize plant magick with your location, choosing native plants when possible. You might try keeping a personal witch's garden, designing it yourself based on your needs, space, and preferences. If you don't have a yard ideal for gardening, work with your space and learn to make the most of it. Consider growing magickal plants indoors or outdoors in flower pots, hanging baskets, and window boxes. A trellis provides lots of vertical growing room for vines in crowded outdoor areas, while an indoor container garden placed on an out of the way small shelf or table adds to the energy and ambiance of the home.

Many magickal plants lend themselves to being worn as natural jewelry to increase magickal power or to boost certain qualities such as psychic awareness. Wrap a fern frond around your wrist for a bracelet to bring out your fun side, twist dandelions around your fingers to make confidence-enhancing flower rings, or use an ivy vine for a belt to invoke a powerful protection.

Plants can also serve as gateways into other realms of consciousness. Sit quietly out in nature and feel the energies of the plants around you. Let go of your human personality and see if you can tune in to nature's botanical essence.

Keep in mind that plants don't need to be picked in order to use them for magick. You can cast spells directly into living plants if you like, invoking powerful earth magick and strengthening your bond with Nature.

Potions and Powders

An infusion of herbs, powdered stones, and other ingredients mixed with water or another liquid, potions can be sprinkled, used to anoint, put in a bath, inhaled, or drunk. Try adding some beauty-enhancing potion to your shampoo or a relaxation blend to your hand soap. For easy potion-making at home or on the go, simply draw a symbol of the qualities you wish to invoke on a piece of paper, and sit a glass of drinking water on top of it. The water will absorb the energies and magickal qualities of the symbol, and when you drink the potion you'll absorb that power for your own.

Magick powders are simply mixtures of dried and powdered herbs or other materials used for a magickal purpose. They can be thrown, placed in sachet-type herbal charms, burned as incense, scattered in the shapes of magickal symbols, and used in countless other ways during spellwork. Try edible powders to spice up your cooking, empowering your spice blends to add magick to the foods you eat. You might also sprinkle some magick powder in your shoes to boost confidence, increase speed, or soothe tired feet.

Potions and powders can also be used to wash or enchant magickal objects. Just choose an appropriate formula and pour it or rub it on the surface of the tool.

You can customize your potions and powders by choosing a signature herb or oil to use in all your blends, adding a small amount to give each recipe your personal trademark. Likewise, formulating your potions and powders with ingredients in tune with your favorite number, element, or season also adds flair. You might want to specialize and become an expert in making certain types of potions and powders; for instance, if you have a special talent for crafting dark moon blends, you'll do well to utilize that gift to its fullest potential.

Magick Wands

Most commonly a charmed branch of wood, a magick wand aids in the amplification and direction of energy during spellwork. By sending magickal power through a wand, the vibration is further purified and strengthened by the magick of the wand itself, and when a spell is released, a wand can help you aim more precisely and release the energy more completely.

Wands are versatile and practical magick tools, and they can be used in ways you might not have tried before. One such way to use your wand is as a handy way to empower threads for use in knot magick. Simply wrap the string around your wand and let it absorb the charge. You can also use your wand to draw symbols in the dirt to strengthen your spells or to communicate messages, and it can even be used to stir potions and mix powders. (However, avoid using your wand to mix ingredients that could negatively alter your magickal tool, such as substances used in strong defensive or banishing magick, or ingredients that would undesirably stain the wood.)

Wands can also be useful in sex spells; try spearing a pomegranate or an apple on the end of your wand to symbolize the sex act. You can even use your wand to relieve bodily discomfort; enchant a wand with healing energies and use it as a magickal back scratcher that will both soothe and rejuvenate you. If you have mobility challenges, try creating a wand that amplifies your magickal power to draw to you what you seek, and use the wand as a handy tool for reaching distant items on your desk or in your cabinets.

Wands can also be employed to quickly clear a tarot deck. Just tap the deck with your wand tip before or after each reading to clear away the energies of any previous readings and get the deck ready for a new querent.

Although store-bought wands are pretty, they're no match for a wand you make yourself. Handcrafting a wand is an enriching experience that results in a very powerful and personalized tool of magick. If you already own a wand, you can still benefit from creating new ones. You can create wands specifically for use in various types of magick or on certain occasions; for example, you might want to craft a wand just for use in defensive magick, or for the sole purpose of celebrating Samhain. You might also create a wand to commemorate a special event or new stage of your life, or a wand designed to harmonize with your elemental affinities, your astrological sign, or your lucky number.

You can obtain materials for your wand in a forest or desert, in a city park, in your own backyard, or even in a parking lot. Look at your surroundings and examine anything that attracts you. When something intrigues you, touch it and feel its energies. If it feels positive and "charged," it will be a helpful ingredient. If you are examining a potential wand, wrap your hand firmly around it. If it's a suitable piece, it will feel like an extension of yourself. You may even feel a surge of energy course through it.

Sticks from holly, oak, maple, ash, aspen, willow, elm, yew, juniper, mesquite, and cypress are particularly well suited for wands, but let your personal feelings guide your selection. Feathers, thorns, crystals, seeds, and other natural items can also be included. Stones can be attached to the outside of your wand, or they can be used powdered or whole as part of the mix you will use in the wandcrafting. Plants found growing within faerie rings (circular growths of mushrooms) add powerful magick to a wand, giving charmswork a boost. To enhance a wand's natural magick, paint it with clays, soils, or berry juices. Incorporate whatever ingredients you like into your wand, but also include some herbs or stones with known potent magickal properties. Some materials of particular merit for use in wands include marigold, honeysuckle, ginger, nutmeg, thyme, cinnamon, allspice, star anise, orange, divine sage, sandalwood, clear and amethyst varieties of quartz, turquoise, and moonstone. All of these have sacred magickal power and are known to open psychic channels.

Once you've gathered your ingredients, decide how you would like to craft your wand. Here are five techniques for making custom-crafted elemental wands that correspond to the natural elements (earth, water, fire, air, and spirit). You should use these instructions for inspiration in formulating your own methods of wandcraft:

Earth Wands

To utilize the element of earth to make your tool, place your wand on a small brown or green cloth. Sprinkle your other ingredients upon it, and rub them thoroughly over the surface of the wand. Wrap up the bundle, and bury it underground for five days during the waxing moon. Bury it at night, and retrieve it during daylight, if possible. If you do not wish to bury your wand, you may place it in a natural dark alcove such as a hole in a tree stump or a moss-covered hollow alongside a stream. Once you retrieve it, you can shake off any loose ingredients, wrap larger pieces onto the wand with a vine or bit of string, or pour a thin mud or paint mixture onto it and let it dry, sealing the loose materials onto the wand.

Water Wands

To craft your wand with the water element, put all your ingredients in a basin of water. Rain, river, or ocean water are potent choices for this method, although any uncontaminated water will do. Allow the mixture to soak for three days, placing it outside after sundown and retrieving it before sunrise each day, keeping it covered in a dark place indoors in the daylight hours. On the fourth morning, take the wand to a sunny place and lay it on a blue cloth to dry.

Fire Wands

Fire, the most dangerous and tricky of the elements to use in wandcrafting, produces a very powerful magickal tool. One technique to craft a fire wand is to wet the exterior of the wood and hold the piece vertically above a candle flame, attempting to burn a small cavity into the inner core of wood. Alternately, you could use a wood-burning tool, or a small metal object such as a tiny Phillips head screwdriver that has been heated in a candle flame, to slowly burn and bore a hole about half to one inch deep into the wand's tip. Be very careful! Make sure your work area is free of any flammable debris, and be sure to protect your body, especially your eyes, hair, hands, and clothing. It's a good idea to wear safety glasses in case a bit of wood goes flying. Once you have prepared the wand with fire, insert your other magickal ingredients into the cavity and seal the hole with a plug of wood, a bit of resin, or a crystal point.

Alternatively, you could wrap the wand and other ingredients in large wet leaves and place the bundle beside a campfire. Once the leaves blacken and start smoking, you can carefully retrieve your wand from the flames using fire tongs or a long stick.

Air Wands

To craft a wand with air, take your ingredients and your wand outdoors, preferably in the daytime so that you can see the effects of wind more clearly. Wave your wand through the air as you sprinkle the ingredients on it with your other hand. Watch the herbs drift through the air toward your wand. Repeat this seven times, or once a day for seven days.

Spirit Wands

To employ the energy of the spirit element to make your wand, wrap the wand up with all the other ingredients you've gathered in a purple cloth. Tie the bundle with nine knots to keep it secure. Place it under your pillow to capture your dream essence from the new moon to the full moon. Do not choose this method if you are prone to nightmares or insomnia, as these conditions will produce an inferior quality wand. On the night of the full moon, untie the cloth and place the wand in the moonlight for at least thirteen minutes.

Tarot Deck

Tarot, that set of 78 cards typically used for fortune-telling, is also an indispensable tool for magick that can be used in spellwork, charms, and ritual.

To help your tarot deck pick up your personal energies, look through it frequently, sleep with it under your pillow, or carry it with you until it feels saturated with your spiritual essence. You might also keep the deck in a cloth bag with a small amount of herbs or stones you find particularly meaningful. Never cease developing and expanding your own ideas about tarot symbolism. The more the cards speak to us, the better we can speak to the cards, using more fully and easily the tarot's versatile magickal power.

Try using tarot to sharpen your psychic abilities; mix the deck into a pile and, without looking, see if you can use your psychic sense to select particular cards. Alternately, you could pick the cards up one by one and see if you can use your ESP to determine the suit.

The tarot can also be used in spirit communication. Simply contact the spirit you wish to talk to and use the cards as a medium for conveying messages back and forth.

Other uses include carrying a card around with you to act as a talisman; for instance, the Lovers card could be carried in order to attract love and romance.

To use the tarot to cast a spell, select relevant cards and place them on your altar in conjunction with the magick's focus. For example, if you need a pay raise but your boss is stingy, you might use tarot to work a spell in order to get circumstances more in your favor. You could choose a card to represent your boss and lay it down, visualizing a clear image of him or her. Next, you might lay down the Four of Pentacles (which can represent clinging to material things) and contemplate the reasons for your boss's stinginess. Then you might reverse the Four of Pentacles so that it now represents generosity, and place it on top of your boss's card. Next, you could cover these cards with the Strength card, magnifying your inner power of courage and boldness and symbolizing that you are on top of the situation. You might finish by placing the Ace of Pentacles above this arrangement to represent wealth, envisioning yourself happy and prosperous. For completion, you might also say an affirmation that expresses the same sentiment.

Tarot can also help us process those painful memories or emotions which if not dealt with, can reduce our inner power and bring down our magick. Begin by laying out a selection of cards to tell the story of what happened. Experience the emotions associated with the circumstance, choose a card to represent your current feelings, and place it to the right of the other cards. Now choose cards to symbolize what you would like to happen in the future, how you would like to be liberated from the present effects of past pain, or how you hope the situation will resolve. Remove all the cards except for these "future" ones, and leave them in place for a day or two to help shift your mindset into a more positive and less burdened outlook.

Tarot is also an extremely useful tool for magickal shortcuts and substitution in both spellwork and ritual. For instance, if you're out of the rose oil called for in a love spell, you could simply set out the Ace of Cups or the Lovers card to invoke similar energies. Likewise, if you're short on time and don't feel like going all out with your usual rituals to draw down deities or call on the elements, you can instead summon these forces by laying out suitable tarot cards on your altar. The High Priestess, the Empress, and the Moon are fitting symbols for goddess energies, while the Magician, the Emperor, and the Sun make nice representations of the god force. The Ace of Cups can summon the element of water and the Ace of Pentacles can be used to represent the powers of earth, while the Ace of Swords and the Ace of Wands can symbolize air and fire.

Tarot's Magickal Attributes: The Major Arcana

To save you time and to jump-start your intuition, here's a handy guide to the magickal attributes of the Major Arcana; take what you like and add to it. Note that what's given here are the qualities of the cards that can be invoked during spellwork; they do not necessarily reflect divinatory interpretations.

The Fool

Good for use in magick to move past worry or doubt, to clear your head before or after rituals, to let go of attachments, or to bring cheer and lightheartedness.

The Magician

Excellent for charms and spells intended to improve magickal skills, magick to manifest success and opportunity, spells to increase ambition and improve leadership, or in spells to help you find magickal tools that suit you. This card can be used in romance magick to represent a male lover.

The High Priestess

Can be used to heighten magickal power, increase ESP, for dream magick, charms to reveal the hidden or discover a lost object, and for spells to bring inspiration. It can be used to represent a female lover in romance spells or as a goddess symbol.

The Empress

Good for fertility charms, boosting femininity and attraction, improving mothering abilities, and for spells intended to bring increase, growth, or abundance. It can also be used in rituals to represent nature or divine feminine essence.

The Emperor

Useful in spells to invoke strength, courage, and willpower, for magick to increase vitality, and in charms to boost sexual energy. It can also act as a god symbol in magick and ritual. Reversed, the card can be used in magick to overcome a negative force of domination, control, or authority.

The Hierophant

Good for spells intended to bring order, balance, stability, or normality. It can be used to represent a marriage, and it can also be employed in ritual to represent an oath. Reversed, it can encourage risk taking and spontaneity, and can be used to break bonds.

The Lovers

Excellent for love and romance magick, and good for spells intended to end quarrels and encourage compassion.

The Chariot

Useful in charms for safe traveling, spells to encourage movement, and in rituals to help the witch plan and prepare for an important action or decision. It can also be used to represent a vehicle or a change of residence.

Strength

Useful in charms and spells to help overcome addiction or other beasts, and for spells to increase confidence and daring. It can also be used for protection and defensive magick.

The Hermit

Useful in bringing peace, acceptance, and solitude; good for charms to find what's lost; and excellent for spells to increase enlightenment. Reversed, it can be used to overcome shyness or loneliness.

Wheel of Fortune

Adds power to most spells, and is excellent for bringing good luck, success, and opportunity. It can also be used to manifest a change of fortune or circumstance, or to represent a cycle or a twist of fate.

Justice

Good for spells intended to set things to right, for spells intended to speed along the effects of karma, and for protective and defensive magick. It can be used to represent legal matters, authority, and fairness.

The Hanged Man

Excellent for invoking a state of heightened spiritual awareness and for aiding in astral projection or entering a trance state; great for meditation; good for spells to calm and soothe irritated nerves, and for charms to create a delay or suspension. It can be used to represent inebriation, and reversed, it can be used to help overcome addiction or indecision.

Death

Great for invoking a major change or upheaval, for spells to transform an existing hierarchy, and for rituals to communicate with the dead or to meditate on and move past grief.

Temperance

Great for bringing balance and moderation, for soothing sorrow or anxiety, and for increasing cooperation and bringing good luck to partnerships. It can also be used to increase reserve, or, reversed, to let go of reserve.

The Devil

Reversed, this card can help overcome addiction, domination, materialism, a shallow physical relationship, or negativity. Upright, it can be used very carefully for protective, positive binding magick, but be clear in your intentions and needs.

The Tower

Can be used to represent a failed plan, an accident, chaos, danger, disaster, or severe depression. Covered with a protective card such as the Ace of Pentacles, and combined with logical and careful action, such misfortune might be prevented or its results lessened. Keep intention positive when using this card.

The Star

Excellent for dream magick, love magick, amplifying magickal energy, spells to increase ESP or replenish the spirit, and charms to make a wish come true.

The Moon

Good for magick intended to keep something secret or concealed, protection magick, spells to increase ESP, spells to absorb and neutralize negativity, and for soothing sorrows. During the waxing moon, it can be used to amplify magickal energy. It is also a goddess symbol. Reversed, this card is useful for spells to discover or overcome untrustworthy influences, or in charms to bring out the truth.

The Sun

Great for purification, banishment, protection, and cleansing spells; also great in healing magick, mood-lifting magick, magick to protect and heal children, and fertility charms. A god symbol, the Sun card amplifies the power of most spells, and is especially potent during summer months.

Judgement

Good for rituals to bring about a reawakening or rejuvenation, in meditations on the cycle of life and death, and in magick to bring something to a close.

The World

Adds power to any spell, great for magick to bring success, wealth, good fortune, and opportunity. This card is also excellent for mood-lifting magick.

EXERCISE

Answer these questions to deepen and expand your ideas regarding magickal tools:

1. How many ways can you think of to use a magick wand?
2. In what ways could you customize the candles you use for rituals?
3. If you were out of the pepper you needed for a banishing spell, what tarot card or cards could you use instead?
4. What new magickal tool would you most like to try? Would you benefit from crafting this tool yourself?
5. Can you think of a new way to use one of the magickal tools you already have?

Taking It Further

Variety is the spice of life and the sugar of magick. We get bored when we do the same old things with the same old tools over and over. Crafting more customized magickal tools and using them in creative ways energizes your practice and encourages you to be bold and innovative, really adding your own insights and skills to the great art of magick.

Challenge yourself to expand your current ideas of magickal tool usage. Pretend you're taking a test and try to think up at least one new way to use each and every magickal tool you own, and then give it a try.

Next, give yourself an even bigger challenge! If you were to invent a brand new magickal tool, what primary purpose would that tool serve? In what other ways might you use it? How do you think such a tool could be crafted? Make a plan and try to execute it; you never know when you might invent a tool that could change the course of magickal culture as we know it.

16

Positive Binding Magick

Studying different perspectives on spellwork will help you progress along your path and give you new ideas to adapt and try. One type of spellcasting many would consider a valuable asset to your magickal arsenal is binding magick.

Binding spells offer a way to magickally seal off and contain energy. Though traditionally associated with cursing, binding spells are nothing to fear, and nothing to shirk. With a little creativity, you can put this powerful form of spellwork to good use to improve your life, protect the planet, and anything else you can think of that might require some extra-strength magick.

Most binding magick seems to operate on one or more of three basic principles:

Principles of Binding Magick

- *Constraint:* Binding the energy, twisting and tying it to itself, in order to restrict its ability to act. This can be accomplished through the physical binding of a symbolic item or through the twisting of symbolic words or images.

- *Containment:* Binding an energy by enclosing it within another form of energy and sealing it off. One way to do this is to create a symbol of the thing you wish to bind and seal it inside a jar or other container.

- *Combination:* Binding an energy by weaving it into and fusing it together with another form of energy. This can be carried out through energy weaving and symbolic actions such as knot tying.

Binding Spells for Positive Use

Here are some examples of positive binding magick to try. Adapt and customize these methods as desired.

"Bind Out the Haters" Spell

This binding spell offers a way to fight back against the forces that bring you down. On a piece of paper, create a list of things that make you feel discouraged. Your list could include things like negative gossip, insults you often hear, self-deprecating speech, anything that makes you feel like giving up. Be as specific as possible in naming the things you wish to bind away from further influencing your emotions.

Once your list is made, employ the constraint principle and cross it out, scribble over it, or use other binding symbols to cover the words. Roll the paper up tightly and seal it with candle wax. Bind it further using the containing principle, securing the rolled paper with a piece of your own hair, or if your hair is short, your hair wrapped around a longer string. Make a strong statement to articulate the binding, such as, "These discouraging forces are bound. They bother me no more!" Keep the paper rolled up and hidden in your home.

You can customize this spell to bind away anything that needs to be kept at bay, and you can add power to the magick by sprinkling the paper with herbs you feel have strong protective, shielding, or soothing properties. If you like, seal the paper up in a jar and decorate the outside of the jar with symbols that represent your confidence, hope, and tenacity.

Ice-Cap Preservation Binding Spell

The earth could certainly use your magickal assistance! One thing to try is the Ice-Cap Preservation Binding Spell, which uses the containing principle of binding magick to help preserve what's left of the ice caps. To work the charm, visualize cords of cold air wrapping around the ice caps as you conjure a feeling of icy hardness. Visualize the cords of cold air spreading to form a white or blue protective web on the surface layer. Say a strong affirmation to seal the binding spell, such as, "The ice is contained and cannot melt. The ice is bound. The ice will last."

Community Improvement Binding Spell

This binding spell can be used to help bring to a community what it needs, be it jobs, food, peace, or a new water tower. Empower one piece of string to represent the community you seek to help. Now empower a second piece of string to act as a symbol of the thing that is needed. Twist the strings together and make a knot in the middle, then a knot at each end. Mentally fuse the two energies together. Through the combining principle, the community's energy is now bound to the energy of what it needs, which should soon be manifest.

As an alternative, you could create an herbal mixture that represents the community as it is now, and choose another herb to represent what the community needs, blending the herbs together and binding the energies into one. You could put the mix in a cloth bag labeled with your town's name, or scatter the mixture all over the city—wherever you think it will do its binding best.

Binding Magick Is Positive Power

Binding magick is one of the strongest, sturdiest, and longest-lasting types of magick there is. Use this form of spellwork when strength counts, when you can't take chances with mediocre magick. Binding magick is not just for cruel jerks who want to curse; it's also for good witches willing to overcome these forces with all their might.

EXERCISE

1. What other positive uses for binding spells can you think of?
2. How could you carry out the constraint principle of binding magick using dough and nails?
3. How could you carry out the containing principle of binding magick using an empty soda bottle and a potion?
4. How might incense making be employed to carry out binding magick based on the combining principle?

Taking It Further

Binding magick is powerful and potent, and it can be used for practical, positive purposes. Experiment with binding spells to seal off addictions, binding spells to improve memory, and binding spells to hold back clutter. Once you've mastered this form of magick, see what grand uses you can put it to. Can you stop a war with a binding spell? Bind a nuclear arms program out of action? Challenge yourself and go for it.

17

Imitative Magick

Imitative magick has been around since primitive man waved his club and cast his first spell. A way of creating in the macrocosm what is imitated in the microcosm, imitative magick is practical, versatile, effective, and a part of nearly every magickal tradition on earth. By learning both traditional and contemporary ways to carry out the principles of imitative magick, you'll gain essential knowledge you can use right now to give your spellwork greater power and flexibility.

Principles of Imitative Magick

Imitative magick is primarily based on one of three principles:

- *Imitating through symbolic Action:* Imitative actions invoke the manifestation of what we mimic. A traditional example is jumping up and down amidst a crop to imitate a growing action and thereby imbue the crop with the same. A contemporary example might be placing a protective symbol over a loved one's photo to imitate the person being covered in protection.

- *Imitating through image:* Images created are made manifest. Cave paintings depicting successful hunting excursions are a primitive example. In modern times, a witch might draw a picture of herself looking affluent in order to manifest more wealth.

- *Imitating through sympathetic attributes:* Magickal objects and ingredients whose attributes are sympathetically linked to what we wish to manifest are employed to create our desires. A traditional example is the use of thorns in defensive potion making, the sharp, painful thorns being sympathetically linked to and therefore able to invoke other sharp, painful terrors. A modern example might be a witch's use of soda pop to add sweetness and pep to a potion.

If you can come up with a way to imitate what you want to create, through actions, images, or sympathetic objects and ingredients, you can perform imitative magick successfully. Try these imitative spells for inspiration in designing your own ways to work this practical form of magick.

Imitative Action Spell

Here's an imitative magick spell you can use to help manifest your biggest dreams. First, think of a goal you want to accomplish. Next, decide what actions you could perform that would imitate the successful achievement of that goal. For example, you might act out catching a winning football pass, signing an autograph, or smiling contentedly.

Imitate the culmination of your goal as best as you can, then send this coded energy into the macrocosm to manifest your dreams.

Make your symbolic actions very specific to who you are and what you want to achieve. Include your mannerisms, posture, and other identifying features in imitative acts to give your magick the power of the personal touch.

Imitative Image Spell

To help create a better world, try this imitative spell. Using paints, pencils, fabric, dough, or other supplies, create an image of the earth. Add symbols and pictures to represent the changes and positive transformations you would like to see come about. Hang the image on your wall, tuck it away in a book, or discreetly leave it in a public place.

You can increase the energy of the spell by anointing the image with the essential oil you most associate with your own magickal power, or by writing phrases around the image detailing exactly what you want to occur.

Sympathetic Imitative Magick Spell

This imitative magick spell relies on sympathetic attributes to forge the connection to the macrocosm. Think of something in your life you wish to be rid of, be it a bad habit, anxiety, or bugs in your cellar. Look around for objects you could use to symbolize the unwanted energy, something that has similar traits or attributes. You could choose based on color, texture, size, shape, magickal energies, or any other characteristics you find significant. If the association makes sense to you, it will work.

Empower the object to act as a symbol of the unwanted energy, then crush it into oblivion. If you like, incorporate magickal tools into the action. In what ways might a wand be useful? How could a magickal knife be used in an imitative way?

Imitative Magick for Flexibility and Power

Imitative magick is especially handy because it is highly effective and really requires no tool other than the imagination. With this versatile skill at your fingertips, you'll be able to design spells for virtually any purpose. You'll also have a means for expressing all the magickal creativity within you that's aching to get out, adding power and greater potential to your personal craft.

EXERCISE

1. What are some examples of imitative magick you've performed?
2. What forms of imitative magick are you best at?
3. What imitative action could you take to help speed something up?

Taking It Further

Imitative magick has a long history, and it is used in some way or another in nearly every magickal tradition you could think of. Study primitive cultures and see if you can identify early excursions into imitative magick. Then look at modern imitative magick practices. Has the art changed much over the years, or are many of the original techniques still in use today? What will you add to the history of imitative magick?

18

Prosperity Magick: Tips, Tricks, and Techniques

Prosperity magick is one of the most popular forms of spellwork, and for good reason: nearly everyone desires wealth. But when we've put forth persistent effort, when we've used our ingenuity, when we've worked our fingers to the bone for years and we still don't have the prosperity we desire, it can start to feel like the universe is against us. We come to believe that it is perhaps our fate, our lot in life, to remain poor. This is nonsense and a limiting belief we might as well be rid of. Prosperity is in reach for everyone, and we all deserve it.

Of course, prosperity is not only an abundance of money. It is the abundant spiritual life as well, a life full of love and happiness, fruitfulness and plenty. But it is the money aspect of prosperity we most often seek through magick, and it is the money aspect that can cause us the most inner conflict.

For spiritually minded people, coming to terms with a desire for wealth can be challenging. We don't want to be greedy; it's simply not in our nature to hoard or to surround ourselves with material possessions. The key is in realizing that money is currency—it's meant to flow. We can use money to achieve great things, relieve suffering, support worthy causes, and create positive change in the world. If money is truly inherently evil, then that's all the more reason we need it in the hands of good, kind people, and magick can definitely help get it there.

More than likely, you've dabbled in wealth-bringing magick in one form or another, and perhaps you were disappointed with the results. When our intent is off or our mindset is contradictory, spells fail, and prosperity magick is quite sensitive to such inconsistencies.

The most important thing to know about wealth-bringing magick is that it is usually imperative to keep your thoughts and feelings focused on abundance and prosperity as you work the charm. Whatever we sow, we reap, and when we perform a money spell while we're focusing on our need, poverty, and lack, we'll attract only more need, poverty, and lack. To successfully manifest money, we must conjure a feeling of wealth. Even if you're flat broke, you have plenty of something, be it grass in your yard, socks, or friends. Focus on what you have in abundance as you engage in prosperity spellwork, and use that feeling as the driving force behind your magick.

Approaches to Prosperity Magick: A New Look

It is always appropriate and preferable to take mundane actions along with the magickal ones, and prosperity magick is no exception. Pursuing our magickal goals in "regular life" ways in addition to ritualistic methods strengthens our commitment and creates opportunities for our spells to succeed. Here are four magickal approaches and their mundane counterparts that can be used as foundations for helping you discover new ways to increase your wealth:

Manifestation Magick

Visualization, intent, sheer energy, and solid steps are utilized to manifest specific realities. Select focused goals that will lead to the prosperity you desire. Visualize yourself attaining each step; see yourself a total success. Give the image emotion and detail. Imagine enjoying ultimate prosperity, and when the feeling is at its height, direct the power into the visualization and send it hurtling into the universe to manifest your dreams in reality.

> *Mundane manifestation:* Define what prosperity means to you, exactly. Make a list of mundane, real-life steps to take to achieve your goals, then take those steps. If you don't know where to begin, start with "step 1: research."

Attraction Magick

Draw to your person the specific things you seek. Create a talisman that symbolizes and will thus attract the prosperity you desire. Personalize the talisman and make use of herbs, stones, colors, numbers, and images. Ingredients could include cinnamon, a coin, and a handwritten note outlining intent, all wrapped up in a green cloth. A talisman can take any form you like. Empower the talisman by connecting with the energetic vibration of wealth and seeing and feeling riches flying straight to you. When the power is at its apex, release it into the talisman. Carry it in your purse or pocket to attract money.

> *Mundane attraction:* Like attracts like, so dress for success and surround yourself with prosperous, successful people. Note money-generating techniques that work for you and repeat, think and walk confidently, and prosperity will be attracted.

Energy Flow/Inertia Magick

Create a power flow that promotes a positive cash flow. Stagnant energy stays stagnant; flowing energy welcomes the new. Increase the flow of wealth into your life by letting small amounts of currency flow and by giving back to the spirits and deities you honor. Make offerings to your patron powers. Concentrate on the free flow of wealth as you dance in inward and outward spirals. See yourself spending and sharing, and see yourself receiving more income. Give thanks and affirm that the current of currency is now flowing.

> *Mundane inertia:* Establish the flow of wealth by freely spending or giving small amounts of money. It's not expensive to be generous. Buying a banana for a hungry stranger, for instance, costs about 30 cents, and the action will get wealth flowing again in your direction.

Multiplication Magick

Multiply and magnify a little into a lot. Wealth can be multiplied through acts of imitative magick. Choose or craft an object to symbolize your current wealth, and manipulate the object in a manner that symbolizes growth or multiplication. Take a coin and write "x 3,000,000" on it. Or choose a plant to symbolize your wealth, and nurture it to grow and thrive.

Wands can also be used for multiplication magick. Place before you some money and direct the energy of the money up through your wand. Visualize and feel the power in your wand multiplying and magnifying the energy of the money, add to this your own energy, and then send it all out through the wand tip and back into the cash.

> *Mundane multiplication:* Examine successes and look for springboards to greater wealth. Network and help others attain success. Think big, invest, capitalize on getting the most out of opportunities, and your wealth will multiply.

Prosperity Magick Rules and How to Bend Them

There are certain rules governing wealth-bringing magick, and most can be bent or broken to suit you. Learning the limitations of prosperity spellwork and how to work around them will enable you to take your money magick to new heights.

Rule 1: You can't create more wealth than you need.

> *How to bend it:* Create more need; expand your idea of what you want money for and what good things you can do with that money.

Rule 2: Your mental/emotional focus should be on wealth, not on need or poverty.

> *How to bend it:* Instead of using a spell, you can directly petition deities for mercy, asking for your great need to be relieved.

Rule 3: Motivation and intent determine results.

> *How to bend it:* You can't. If you want greater wealth for reasons of selfishness, greed, or domination, you might get the wealth, but you'll also get the repercussions of your true agenda. If, however, you have positive, kind reasons for desiring wealth, you'll get your material wealth along with the return of the joy and love surrounding your goal.

Correspondences for Prosperity Magick

Familiarizing yourself with symbolic correspondences useful in prosperity magick will give you more options for crafting effective spells. How ironic it is that so many wealth-bringing spells call for a slew of expensive ingredients! It is never necessary to spend money on supplies for a wealth-bringing charm. Learn different ways to achieve the same ends, and use ingredients and components you already have or can make for free. Here are some elements you can incorporate into any form of prosperity magick, making it easier to design your own spells or to choose effective substitutions and adaptations for existing spells:

- *Colors*: green, gold, or silver for money, growth, and general prosperity, purple for power, orange for attraction, brown for stability and substance, red for energy

- *Symbols*: coins, dollars, cornucopias, arrows, acorns, dollar signs, pentacles, the sun, the moon, infinity sign
- *Herbs*: cinnamon, nutmeg, cedar, basil, allspice, patchouli, frankincense, pine, clove, orange, holly, oak
- *Foods*: apples, grapes, beans, pomegranates, bread, honey, collard greens
- *Numbers*: 3 or 7 for luck and power, 9 for multiplying wealth, 10 for abundance

Stones: agate, jacinth, jade, turquoise, clear quartz

Customizable Prosperity Spells

Here are a few customizable spells you can use as inspiration for crafting your own creative wealth-bringing magick:

The Dance of Prosperity

This spell uses attraction magick to quickly increase your wealth. Take nine shiny coins outside and dance around in a wide clockwise circle as you scatter the coins, tossing one freely into the air at east, south, west, and north, and then on your second pass, at northeast, southeast, southwest, and northwest. As you toss each coin, visualize yourself gleaming with wealth and generously sharing your prosperity with others. Imagine you are tossing coins to all the people and causes you wish to support. Now visualize yourself standing in the middle of the circle looking very prosperous, and cast the final coin at your image. Choose your own words to express your belief in yourself as a prosperous person who attracts resources, then release the energy. Keep the central coin to carry with you as a money-bringing talisman, and give the others away.

Try adapting this spell by using other symbols of wealth such as acorns or evergreen sprigs, or by changing the imitative actions, for example, walking forward or uphill rather than dancing in a circle. You might also experiment with alternative spell release techniques, such as finding out how well the spell performs when you deposit the magickally charged coins in your bank account post-ritual.

Money Multiplier Candle Spell

Choose a green, gold, or silver candle as the focal point of your spell. If you like, anoint the candle with patchouli, frankincense, or another wealth-bringing oil to help amplify the charm. Select a symbol to carve into the candle. You might choose a dollar sign, a plus sign, a multiplication sign, or the symbol of a deity of prosperity. Focus your thoughts on the multiplication of wealth as you carve the symbol into the wax. Visualize the money in your wallet rapidly expanding. Think of abundance, count your blessings, and when the feeling is at its height, send the energy into the candle, visualizing it glowing with a golden, red, or purple light. Now drip wax around the candle, making several large dots. In each wax circle, carve the same symbol you used on the candle. Now choose some words to affirm your intent to carry out multiplication magick, saying something such as, "Many manifest from the one. So too may my dollars be multiplied!" With that, snuff the candle flame between your fingers, imagining that you are catching a hundred dollar bill.

You can customize this spell by making your own specially designed candle to use, putting intention, symbolic shape, and appropriate herbs into the mix. Or add a bit of your favorite element, using a floating candle in a bowl of water, smearing earth on or around the candle, blowing gently on the flame to invoke the wind, or using a red candle to further symbolize fire itself.

Community Prosperity Inertia Charm

Here's a charm to increase both the spiritual and material prosperity of your community. Go through your couch cushions or other out of the way areas and collect any coins or dollars you find. Also choose a piece of clothing and a food item. Charm the stuff by touching it and imbuing it with an energy of love, wealth, and swiftness. Now take a walk through your town, giving the coins and other items to people you see who might need them or making a donation to a local shelter. Be friendly and walk with an aura of love and prosperity, letting it shine on the people you meet and rub off on the places you go.

Alternatively, you could make an affordable shopping excursion to get prosperity magickally flowing through your town, spending a charmed dollar or two here and there, wherever you feel it's most needed. You could also choose to create magickal inertia by helping out through the power of your own hands, planting edibles in public areas, or organizing a full-fledged community garden or free box.

Like Money in the Bank

Now that you've examined the principles, correspondences, and customization of prosperity magick, you'll be able to see this type of magick in a new light that will bring a fresh glow to your spellwork. You know what you need to know to have another try at making that big dream come true; believe in yourself and give it a go! Understand the principles, familiarize yourself with the correspondences, and make each spell your own, and you'll be well on your way to greater prosperity.

Exercise

1. Define prosperity and success.
2. Do you deserve to be wealthy? Why or why not?
3. In a primitive tribe, what would your role be, and what is this role's career equivalent in modern times? Is that a source of wealth you'd like to look into?
4. Who has achieved goals you'd like to achieve, and can you imitate and improve the techniques they used to get there?
5. Set a small goal with a three-month time frame, and a big goal with a three-year time frame. What's the first step to achieving each goal?
6. What are some types of magick you can use to increase prosperity?

Taking It Further

In addition to manifestation magick, inertia magick, multiplication magick, and attraction magick, from what other angles could you approach a spell to increase prosperity? What are the symbols, herbs, stones, and colors you personally associate with wealth? Is there a limit to how much wealth you'd like to attain? Study ancient methods of prosperity magick, including the practice of sacrifice and the use of amulets. Research mainstream moneymaking strategies as well, picking up tips and techniques that could work for you. By taking a well-rounded approach to achieving prosperity, you will be able to attain the wealth you desire.

19

Love Magick: Spells and Secrets

L ove spells manifest love, which can be employed in countless ways to create an amazing existence. Too often, love spells are focused on gaining the attentions of a suitable suitor, but that's just a small portion of the spectrum. Love magick can help us win love, repel beasts, turn frogs into princes, gain self-acceptance, and even get intimate with our patron deities. Learn the principles and correspondences of love magick, and you'll be able to craft and cast this type of spell for maximum effect.

Principles of Love Magick

Most love magick operates on one of three basic principles:

- *Attraction magick:* Drawing a loving energy toward a specific destination, be it person, place, or object. One way to carry out attraction magick is through the like-attracting-like principle underlying imitative forms of magick. For instance, if you wanted to attract love to your life, you could create a talisman empowered with loving energies that match the love you seek, perhaps marking it with a love symbol and anointing it with an appropriate oil. The talisman, now perfectly patterned and coded to a loving vibration, will attract more of that loving vibration straight to you.

- *Combining magick:* Weaving or mixing together a loving energy with the energy of the person, place, or thing on which the spell is to act. One way of combining energies is with binding magick. For example, for a spell to cause a cold-hearted person to grow more loving, you could obtain one of the person's hairs and knot this together with a pink thread empowered with a loving energy. The person's energy is now fused to love, and they will hopefully grow a little nicer.

- *Containing magick:* Literally encasing a person, place, or thing within a container of loving energy, thereby keeping the spell's target within a controlled only-love-may-enter environment. One way to carry out containing magick requires nothing but your own magickal power. For example, suppose you want to send a faraway depressed friend some love and protection. You could start by raising the loving energies within yourself to an intense frequency. Then visualize the target of your spell clearly as you project your loving energies directly to them, seeing in your mind's eye the power of your magick surrounding and containing your friend in an orb of protective love.

Correspondences for Love Magick

Here are some magickal associations you can use for ideas as you custom-craft your own love spells:

- *Colors:* pink for soft, romantic love; red or purple for passionate love; white for pure, innocent love; blue for bright and happy true love

- *Symbols:* hearts, interlocking circles, glyphs formed from combined initials

- *Herbs:* rosemary, basil, cinnamon, rose, thyme, vanilla

- *Foods:* apples, peaches, apricots, cherries

- *Numbers:* 2 for union, 6 for perfect beauty

- *Stones:* emerald, aquamarine

Love Magick's One Rule

Love magick has one rule, and one rule only: Casting a spell to make a specific person fall in love with another specific person is not a viable option; it simply won't work. To control is not the nature of love, and magick intended to force another to love you will bring about not love, but a relationship of selfish gain and confinement.

While it's perfectly fine to magickally send your own love to a specific person of your affections, trying to coerce that person into returning the love can lead to crazy karmic consequences. But although a love spell can't brainwash your hot crush into becoming your devoted love slave, it could still potentially entice that person or someone even more compatible into checking you out.

Remember that love spells are meant to work softly and subtly. They're not intended to scan the singles ads for you and force "Hot and Lonely in Houston" to give you a call. With or without magickal help, if you are projecting your ideal self, you will attract your ideal mate. Love spells simply overpower any obstacles that would otherwise delay the meeting.

A Word to the Witch

Being shy about real love is one of the saddest and stupidest mistakes a witch can make. Yet, many of us have a story to tell of a precious love lost. In most magickal practice, it's best to not speak of a spell once it has been performed. Perhaps this is part of the reason so many witches have successfully performed various love charms, found and fallen completely in love with someone worthy and wonderful, and then lost it all by failing to put those feelings into words. Shying away from acknowledging shared sacred love directly can give a false impression of indifference. Don't be an idiot—when you experience real love, be open and honest about how you feel. Your love magick will work, so don't blow it!

Love Potion #1

To gain some luck in meeting your true love, try this simple brew that operates on the principles of attraction magick. Place a clean, chemical-free rose petal, preferably from a pink or red rose, into a cup of hot water. Conjure a clear mental image of your ideal self. See yourself as radiant, successful, sexy, and loving. Drink a small sip, taking care to not swallow the rose petal. Send forth a feeling of deep love. Add another rose petal to the cup and conjure an image of your ideal true love. See the person's eyes and feel their essence. Take a sip and feel the person loving you. Swirl the contents of the cup until the two rose petals come together. Place a third petal over these and say something in your own words to the effect of, "I'm here, my love. Come to me." Take a sip and send out a feeling of giddy excitement. Pour the remaining contents of the cup onto the ground in a circle or heart shape surrounding you, and hold the rose petals in your hand. Repeat your chosen mantra and send forth an intense loving energy as you picture yourself with pink or white light radiating from your core. Keep some of the light with you to act as a magnet for your true love, and toss the rose petals freely into the air. If you prefer, tie the rose petals up in a piece of cloth to make a charm to keep in your pocket or purse. You could also opt to drink the entirety of the brew and skip the part where you spill out the remaining liquid. Or you could choose to pour out all the liquid, perhaps forming words that express the love you truly desire.

This magick usually works rather quickly, so make sure you look your best and are radiating confidence at all times.

Love Potion #13

- 3 parts rosemary
- 1 part allspice
- 2 parts cinnamon

Use this potion to induce romantic dreams, particularly if you wish to dream of a faraway love. With intent, steep the herbs in a cup of hot water for thirteen minutes. Dip a piece of your jewelry or a piece of string into the potion. Put on the jewelry or tie the potion-soaked string around your left wrist to wear while sleeping, using the principles of combining magick to fuse the dream-inducing energies to your body. With a little luck, you'll be able to hook up with your known or as-yet-unknown love interest in the dream world.

This potion can also be used to have a lucid dream where you can spend some time with a deity or spirit. Just add an ingredient to the mix symbolizing the force or spirit with whom you wish to communicate.

For another way to customize this blend, you could sew the same herbal combination into a small pillow that could be used to the same effect. If the mixture is used in this way and your intent is to dream about a specific person, the magick can be strengthened by including a photo or another token representing the individual you wish to dream about.

Get Along Spice

- 1 part pepper
- 1 part sage
- 1 part salt
- 2 parts rosemary

Use this magick powder to season foods or sprinkle it around the house to end disputes and encourage love through the principles of containing magick. When you empower the herbs, think of what you love about everybody and how much you want everyone to have fun. Send a joyous, peaceful light into the spice, then imagine this power surrounding your loved ones, containing them in a calm and caring energy. This mix tastes delicious on roasted potatoes or in stuffing.

For a variation, add affirmations to the mix, saying soothing, reassuring words as you blend the spice. You might also choose to empower the spices with music; simply place the herbs near the stereo and put on some feel-good tunes.

Love-Bringing Charm

To bring romantic candidates out of the woodwork, try this bit of attraction magick. Tie up three clover flowers inside a small circle of white natural fabric. Visualize yourself surrounded by attractive suitors. Take your feeling of irresistible charm and cast it into the flower bundle held in your left hand. Do a sweeping motion in the air with your wand or hand, as if gathering new friends toward you. Tap the bundle with your wand or fingertips and send a jet of blue or pink light into it as you say, "Trust," and emit a calming energy. Carry the bundle with you for up to three moon cycles. If there is a person you already know who is your perfect match, the charm will work in very mysterious ways.

If you like, customize this spell by using a different type of flower or herb or a different color of fabric. For another variation, place the three clover flowers in your bath water instead, adapting the other parts of the spell to suit.

Lover's Toast

- 2 parts rosemary
- 1 part basil

Blend ingredients into 1/4 cup of butter over low heat. Stir seven times clockwise, three stirs counterclockwise, then seven stirs clockwise, and so forth, until the mixture is melted and becoming fragrant. Inhale the aroma and conjure a feeling of lighthearted joy. Release this energy as a lavender light flowing into the blend. Pour over two slices of toast and share with a loved one to promote love and happiness.

You can also try adding a visualization to the cooking process, thinking of your lover's kiss as the butter melts and the spices heat.

Intrigue Enchantment

Here's a charm to use when you're out and about and looking for love. If you wish to attract the attentions of a certain person, try this powerful enchantment. Conjure a deep feeling of pure love and direct this as a soft flow of white light toward the person of your desire. Now see yourself as the very image of attraction and charm. A violet light emanates gracefully from your brow. Look over at your love interest. If the person makes eye contact, visualize yourself parting some red curtains and flash a dazzling smile. If they aren't looking yet, visualize the orange light of your sexual chakra, located at the pelvis, radiating vibrations toward the person. Release a feeling of unhindered love, and let your eyes portray nothing but mystery and a graceful joy. The target of the charm will be drawn to you like a moth to a flame, but keeping them there is up to you!

An adaptation could include a more specific visual image: instead of visualizing yourself as simply "attraction itself," try picturing yourself in your mind as either the High Priestess or Magician tarot card, or as a sexy star you admire. For another way to modify this quickly cast charm, develop a longer spell-length version.

Loving Influence Charm

To produce a bodily flash of love and light, bringing a loving influence and good luck to any situation or to the world at large, cast this charm. Concentrate a loving energy within your brow and release it in a quick three-blink flash through your eyes. See yourself as luminous, positively glowing with vibrant light, as you cast the charm.

For a variation, try making a sound or specific movement as you release the magick.

Love Magick Is Lovely

With love magick, we can really do some important magickal work. The same techniques that can be used to increase love in the individual's life can be applied on a larger scale, bringing greater love to the entire world. Aim higher than just a date for Saturday night. Use love magick in the biggest, brightest, best ways you can dream of.

EXERCISE

1. What do you think is the highest purpose that could be achieved with a love spell?
2. What is the one rule of love magick? Would you break this rule? Why or why not?
3. What symbols, herbs, and other magickal ingredients do you personally associate with loving energies?

Taking It Further

When we're not our best selves, we have no chance of attracting or producing the best love. What can you do right now to reflect more of who you really are? What do you want a mate to love about you? Let these qualities shine, and give them not only to your lover, but also to the world through your large scale love magick.

20

Advanced Defensive Magick

There are certain forces that intend to gather up energy and direct it into enslavement. In contrast to the good witch who gratefully asks the living energy to help bring about a desired change, baneful forces greedily seek to entrap and command. This way is folly, as all energy is of one creation, and the perceived confinements that separate energy into seemingly distinct groupings are an ephemeral illusion, a grand and blessed trick played on us by magickal power itself. Just like pollution dumped in one part of a river affects the whole ecosystem, those who hurt just for the sake of it dirty up their own environment with their psychic garbage.

Do not fear these forces. The magickal power within you is sacred and eternal. Fight back. As positive and light as we might like our magick to be, let's face it: sometimes you've just got to take out the trash to protect your own environment. Let's take a look at the principles on which defensive magick operates.

Principles of Defensive Magick

Defensive magick often operates on one or a combination of four basic principles. Do any of these descriptions remind you of your natural visualizations during protective or defensive magick?

Containing
Surrounding the danger with an inescapable energy and sealing it off. One way to accomplish this is through imitative actions or image magick.

Binding
Binding and tying up the threatening party's energy so that they are restricted from certain actions specified by the spellcaster. One way to do it is through the constraint principle of binding magick.

Banishing
Driving outward and away, expelling the unwanted energy. This can be accomplished through charms and other magicks that send forth a blast of power.

Shielding
Building a shield of impenetrable, protective energy around what you wish to protect to seal out the threat. One way to produce it is through visualization and energy weaving.

Correspondences for Defensive Magick

Use these associations to help you craft your own forms of advanced defensive magick.

- Colors: black to bind, shield, or contain; white to protect; gray to neutralize
- Symbols: pentacles for general protection, x's to cross out threats, downward pointing arrows for halting and holding, counterclock-

wise spirals for undoing or trapping

- Herbs: black pepper, red pepper, bay, salt, cumin, pine, aconite, mandrake root
- Foods: pineapple, hot peppers, garlic, onion
- Numbers: 9 to bind, 13 for undoing, 4 to block in or shield
- Stones: jet, onyx, amethyst

Serious Spells for Serious Defense

You've got your own sense of ethics; I'm not going to preach mine any further. If the need arises and defensive magick is called for, here are some spells you might find useful. Feel free to personalize, but keep in mind that these are serious spells with serious consequences; be sure the principles, symbolism, and motivation behind your adaptations are right on.

Be aware that magick of this sort sometimes works in a rather ugly fashion, as it can cause karma to quickly catch up with the threatening individual. You won't be able to control the particulars of the outcome, as this is not your part in the work. You are merely seeking to rid yourself of the person, and it's up to the powers that be to design the way.

It's important to forgive the dangerous person you are averting and let go of any grudges before using strong defensive spells. That way, if a bad fate does befall your foe, you won't be tempted to think it was your doing.

Tossing the Egg

If you need a person to be completely out of your life forever, consider this spell. Go outside alone with an uncooked egg and a black writing utensil. Hold the egg in your hand and write the person's name on it. If you know their full name, write it all. Get a clear image of the person in your mind as you write the name.

Drop the writing utensil on the ground, and hold the egg in your dominant hand, still visualizing the person you need to get away from you. Include the fear and negativity surrounding the person as part of the visualization. Now see the person steadily shrinking in size, until they fit into the egg you are holding. The egg has now become a symbol of your enemy.

Visualize black threads wrapping around the egg. Articulate out loud or mentally that the person will be out of your life forever, identifying them by name. For instance, you could say, "Mr. Bad Guy is out of my life forever. He is bound and can no longer come in contact with me. With this egg, his influence will be broken and he will be out of my life forever." Picturing the person as very small, about two inches tall, and wrapped tightly in the egg bound in black threads, gently toss it so that it rolls on the ground at least eight or nine feet away from you. Fling away your tiny enemy as you toss the egg. Toss it very softly so that it doesn't crack. Don't look to see where it landed, and don't return. Dispose of the writing utensil used in the ritual. When an animal breaks into the egg, the person will be out of your life forever.

Needle, Thread, Paper

If you need to render someone powerless so that he or she can't harm you, consider performing this bit of magick. Write the person's name on a piece of paper and fold it nine times. As you fold the paper, visualize the person folding in on him- or herself until he or she becomes a tiny cube. Take a needle threaded with black string or with a strand of your foe's own hair and sew the folds of the paper together with nine stitches, as you picture the person who is now a little cube being flattened out, until the person is just a tiny scrap.

Next, take the paper and bury it deep in the ground away from your home. Bury around this nine burnt matches, encircling the place where the paper is buried. Say, "You are bound. You are powerless. You can harm me no more."

Covering with Wax

If you want to create a barrier so that a person's negative energies can no longer influence or affect you, try this spell. Write the person's name as small as possible on a piece of thick paper. Light a black candle. Get a clear image of the person in your mind and visualize this image atop the candle flame. Picture the person's negativity being consumed by the flame as you steadily replace the image with a bright white light.

When you see mostly white light and the person is just barely visible, take the candle in your hand and drop nine drops of wax on the name you have written, so that the wax completely covers the writing. Flood your mind with bright white light and project this force to blast away any lingering trace of the person in your visualization.

The spell is now complete except for cleanup. Crumple the paper and throw it out.

Tips for Better Defensive Magick

- Salt and pepper are potent magickal ingredients in any protective, defensive, or purifying spell. Salt is used mainly for basic protection and general purification, whereas pepper acts more specifically to target and expel distinct negative entities.
- It's often best to work defensive magick alone and in the dark.
- Put the spellcasting out of your mind once the magick has been performed.
- Once your spell is cast, know that you will be safe. Stop focusing on your enemy, but remain watchful.

Stand Up and Defend!

Magick is powerful stuff, and we're meant to use it for powerful stuff. When you see or hear of someone or something under threat, use your magick for good and see what you can do to help. You'll be surprised at the advantage that magick has over muscle, and you'll give your spellcasting skills a workout that will have you sprinting even further along your magickal path.

EXERCISE

1. In what situations do you think advanced defensive magick would be justified?
2. If you were facing a serious threat, to what extent would you be willing to use your magick?
3. What do you feel is your strongest form of defensive or protective magick?

Taking It Further

Defensive magick is a valuable art. It can literally save your life. What specific techniques of magickal defense would you like to master? Who or what on earth could you help with defensive magick, right now? In what ways can you practice and hone the skills you already have? Learn what you need to know, decide who or what needs defending, and do it.

21

Mood-Lifting and Luck Magick

Whether down in the dumps or down on our luck, we all could use a pick-me-up now and then. With mood-lifting and luck magick, you can find it. Let's explore mood-lifting magick, then we'll take a look at how to change your luck for the better.

Mood-Lifting Magick

With serious grief or depression, professional counseling services and other treatment options or support services are usually needed. But if what you're experiencing is simply a mild to moderate case of the blues, mood-lifting magick can help bring on a real smile fast.

Principles of Mood-Lifting Magick

Mood-lifting magick primarily operates on one of two basic principles:

- *Absorbing negativity:* The mood-lifting formula absorbs and neutralizes negative emotional energy. One example is a jet stone used to absorb negativity and help stave off depression.
- *Infusing positivity:* The mood-lifting formula infuses the user with a rush of positive emotional energy. One example is a sunwater potion that imbues the drinker with a solar energy that amplifies happiness.

What other ways of accomplishing mood-lifting magick can you think of? How might you carry out the two principles described above?

Correspondences for Mood-Lifting Magick

Use these associations to design your own mood-lifting spells.

- *Colors:* yellow or blue for happiness, white for positive energy, gray for neutralizing negativity
- *Symbols:* suns, happy faces, upward pointing arrows, flowers, clockwise spirals
- *Herbs:* rosemary, basil, lavender, dandelion, marigold, sage, vanilla
- *Foods:* sunflower seeds, peach, strawberry, watermelon
- *Numbers:* 3 and 7 for good feelings and good fortune
- *Stones:* turquoise, citrine, emerald, and aquamarine to infuse positivity; jet and hematite to absorb negativity

Mood-Lifting Spells and Brews

When doing magick to lift spirits, make sure your posture is confident and content. If you're stirring up a happiness brew with slumped shoulders and a dismal frown, your energies will be locked into that feeling and you will be unable to project the positive energy necessary to effectively make the potion.

Here are some formulas to try. See if you can identify the principles of mood-lifting magick (absorbing/neutralizing negativity or infusing positivity) behind each method. What might you add to make these spells and brews more personal and potent?

Sunwater: A drink of this potion will produce a feeling of happiness. Set a vessel of water outside at dawn and empower it to receive the happiness-inducing virtues of the sun. If you like, draw an image of the happiness you want the potion to invoke and sit the container of water on top of this image to brew. Retrieve the water in late afternoon, knowing that it is now brimming with solar energy.

Peace potion: Collect some tears in a jar and place in this a piece of turquoise, a jet stone, and one dandelion bloom. Anoint your forehead with three drops of the mixture to mellow sorrows and bring peace.

For a more custom brew, add an extra ingredient of your choice to neutralize sorrowful energies.

Happiness vapor: Heat a vessel of water and place within it a generous amount of lavender and chamomile. Inhale the steam to bring happiness and calm your nerves. If you're a frugal witch, strain the herbs out of the water when you're done, and leave them to dry out. You can use this again for things like potpourri, but keep in mind that the herbs will be already depleted of a large measure of their magickal energy and will need to be re-empowered before second use.

To give this spell the personal touch, utter out loud and let go of one of your worries with each exclamation.

Pick-me-up spell: Take a clear or smoky quartz or amethyst crystal and lay it on your chest. Think of all your woes and worries and send them out of you and into the crystal. Shake the stone in the air a few times and set it aside.

Now take a piece of rose quartz or turquoise and lay it on your forehead. Feel calming, joyful energies flowing out of the stone and into your body. This spell will greatly heighten your mood, and keeping the turquoise or rose quartz with you for a few days can enhance the effect.

The crystal you use to absorb negative energies will need to be cleansed with salt and sunlight or another energy-clearing method after this work, before it is used for any other magick and before carrying it on your person.

Try customizing this spell to make it even more effective. Choose your own combination of stones for which you share special affinities.

Luck Magick

It's true—joy is the foundation of good luck. When we feel down, we are; we drag ourselves and our energy into the dirt along with our luck. So what is this "lucky" stuff? It's the excitable and active magickal energies you attract and amass around you, and the more joy you feel, the better is your luck. Now that you've got more magickal tricks for feeling joyful, it's time to try some luck-boosting magick. Let's take a look at the principles underlying this form of spellwork.

Principles of Luck Magick

Luck magick generally works by doing one of two things, or both:

- *Removes obstacles:* The luck magick clears away any psychic or mundane blocks that delay you in being at the right place at the right time. One example is a talisman used to ward off misfortune.

- *Increases opportunities:* The luck magick sets circumstances in your favor so opportunities will be a way of life. An example is a lucky charm that is empowered to attract useful allies.

Correspondences for Luck Magick

Use these associations as inspiration for your own luck magick.

- *Colors:* green, gold, silver, your favorite color
- *Symbols:* clovers, horseshoes, stars

- *Herbs:* clover, star anise, thyme, nutmeg, vanilla, allspice, ginger
- *Foods:* oranges, starfruit, black-eyed peas
- *Numbers:* 3, 7, 13, your lucky number
- *Stones:* emerald, turquoise, moonstone

Super Lucky Magick Spells

Here are some general luck-bringing charms to increase opportunity and remove obstacles. Remember, it's up to you to take advantage of any magickally fortunate circumstances. Be ready to work after completing the spell.

Magick Powder

Mix together equal parts ginger, nutmeg, finely grated orange peel, and allspice. Empower the herbs with a bright, confident energy. Whenever you have a special wish you would like granted, use a bit of the powder to trace a symbol of your wish onto your body. Visualize your wish coming true, then dust off the powder, making a polite request for help.

As a variation, magick powder can also be sprinkled to charm buildings or outside areas with good luck, although the charm does not last long. You can also personalize the blend by adding an ingredient to act as your energetic signature, an herb that is special to you for its astrological associations, its magickal attributes, or anything else that thrills you. Customizing luck magick always makes it extra potent.

Bound to Luck Up Spell

If you've had a lot of bad luck and you want to wrap your hands around some good fortune, wrap one of your hairs around the stem of a growing, healthy rose. Spirits of fortune will recognize this as a call for assistance. Keep up with watering and caring for the rose plant, as the energies upon which you are calling prefer the witch to show some respect and mutual compensation in his or her craft.

To take this spell further, design your own preliminary rituals for connecting with the energies of the rose and asking it to deliver your message to the forces of fortune. Experiment with ways you can use magick to support the plant's growth, and your luck will thrive along with the rose.

Acorn Charm

Hold an acorn in your hand and visualize it growing into a large oak tree. Empower the acorn with positive vibrations and magnetism. Say, "In you are the seeds of fortune. May you grow tall and fast!" You can tie the acorn to a green, brown, white, or red string and wear it as a necklace, or simply carry it in your pocket as a good luck talisman.

For a more powerful charm, anoint the acorn with a favorite blend of essential oil and decorate it with meaningful symbols or words.

Lucky Star Charm

For good luck in achieving a goal, take seven pieces of star anise and sprinkle them with vanilla extract. Empower them by magnifying their helpful and creative energies. Now make your wish for better luck and cast this energy into the spice. Tie it up in a silver or bright blue cloth and carry it with you whenever you plan on taking a step toward achieving your goal. This charm is especially effective for job interviews or for landing creative opportunities.

To personalize your charm, write down on a slip of paper exactly what your wish is, including your full name and any lucky symbols or numbers. Tie the paper up in the cloth with the rest of the charm, and enjoy a super-lucky fast-acting magick.

Happy and Lucky

Mood-lifting and luck magick are great tools that work together. Luckiness increases happiness, and happiness increases luck. Don't let melancholy moods or fortune's cruel twists bring you down. Pull out your magick tricks, and good times will soon be in store.

EXERCISE

1. What makes you feel happy? How could you incorporate a symbol of its essence into your mood-lifting magick?
2. What's the luckiest you've ever been? Is there a symbol, herb, sound, or image you associate with this occurrence that you could use in your luck magick to re-invoke a fortunate atmosphere?

Taking It Further

What other ways of casting mood-lifting magick can you think of? How might you produce a potion that induces a playful mood? What do you think about lucky charms? Are these common tokens examples of real magick in the hands of the masses? Research lucky charms from around the world, and study the attributes of plants used to boost spirits. You'll soon have a body of knowledge you can draw on to craft your own effective, personalized spells that will best lift your mood and kick-start your luck.

22

Exploring Abilities

So what if you're not the world's best wand waver or you can't light a charcoal block without burning your fingers? We each have our own abilities and aptitudes, and learning how to play to our strengths makes our weaknesses less relevant. Can't make potions very well, but you're a pro at herbal sachets? Then go with the herbs and skip the potions. Likewise, if you're an expert at candle magick, making that the primary medium in your most important spells will help assure your success. When we know what we're good at, and also what we're not so good at, we can design our spellcraft to take advantage of our strengths, and we can practice and work on developing those skills we lack. It's time to explore your spellcasting abilities and experience the thrill and new opportunity of discovering magickal talents you never knew you had. Let's get started.

Spellwork Aptitude Exercise

Here's an exercise to help you discover your aptitude for certain types of spellwork. You'll find out if you have a knack for love, wealth, protection, or healing magick, and you can focus on this area to make your magick super effective.

You'll need cinnamon, bay, rosemary, and lavender for this exercise, or any other two sets of herb pairings that share two different attributes. Start with the bay and cinnamon. These herbs both have properties of protection and psychic power. Using your best empowering method, try to charge up both herbs to bring out the protective energy. Check to see which herb you were able to charge up the most, and rate the level of magickal power you've imparted on a scale of one to three. Now empower these herbs to bring out the psychic power attribute, and log your results in the same manner. Now do the same with the rosemary and lavender, this time empowering the herbs for healing and then for love. What are your results? Are you better at conjuring protective energy than you are at conjuring psychic power energy? Was empowering the herbs with a loving energy a cinch? You can use this information to help pinpoint the spell categories you're best at, and you might also discover more about your herbal affinities in the process.

To adapt this exercise for skill building, practice switching the herbs back and forth between attributes. For example, with the rosemary and lavender, you could alternate rapidly between bringing out the loving energy and then the healing energy. This will improve your ability to overpower present energy patterns with your own magickal code.

How's Your Wandwork?

This exercise tests your ability to effectively use a wand. You can adapt this same exercise to test your skill with magick knives and staves as well. Choose an ordinary rock from outside, something that doesn't have a lot of natural charge. For example, a sandstone or piece of granite with a relatively dull energy would be preferable over a quartz crystal positively pulsating with energy. Sit the stone in front of you, not empowering it in any way beforehand. Now pick the energy you would like to send into the rock, be it a loving energy or a dark and disastrous energy. Select an energy you are good at conjuring. Once you've made your selection, point your wand at the stone and try to send the chosen energy through the wand and into the stone. Check the stone to see if it seems charged. Did it work?

You can adapt this exercise into a skill-building activity, too. Just repeat the experiment, each time standing farther away from the stone. How far away can you be and still send a blast of power out of your wand? If you find you can do this from ten feet away or more, you'll know you have a special aptitude for wand use. If, on the other hand, it's difficult to accomplish unless the wand is actually touching the stone, either you need a new wand or you'll know this is a skill that needs practicing.

Transfiguration Test

This exercise offers a way to build and test your transfiguration abilities—that is, your skill in causing changes in the physical makeup of an object through the use of magickal power. By intentionally imparting a new structural pattern to the magickal power inherent in an object, it's possible to alter the object's physical properties. Don't believe it? Try this.

Take two ice cubes of equal size. Connect to the magickal energy within one of the ice cubes. It is clear energy, without attribute and ready for your instructions. You'll want to code the energy to make it hard, cold, and impervious. Methods you might employ include conjuring a feeling of extreme cold, thinking of ice and snow and imagining it until you can feel it. You could then blast that energy into the ice cube, tapping it with a wand or your fingertips. The moment the cold energy goes into the ice cube, think of that energy growing harder, spreading from the center of the ice cube outwards to form a very hard, very cold, impervious shell around the outside surface of the ice cube. Think of the ice as impervious to the effects of heat, think of the ice staying intact. The ice will need to be charmed quickly so that there won't be a lot of melting time between taking the ice out of the freezer and actually starting the experiment. It's meant to be a quick charm, a fast flash that makes it happen.

As soon as one of the ice cubes is transfigured to be harder and colder and slower to melt, take both ice cubes outside and set them down on the sidewalk or in the grass, side by side with a few inches in between them. You'll need a warm day, or as a variation, you can do the experiment indoors with the ice cubes in a pan, heating it with the stove on low. Is the ice cube you transfigured the last to melt?

A similar exercise you can do to sharpen your transfiguration skills is to transfigure a pot of water to be fast-boiling, and then time how long it takes it to boil. Be sure to use the same level of heat, the same pot, and the same amount of water each time. You'll have better results if you do these experiments alone. We're allowed to bend the rules of physical reality a little more when no one is looking! Keep a record and try to improve your times.

Potions Practice

This exercise tests your potion-making abilities. You'll need two seeds of the same variety, some spring water, a clear glass container, and a green glass container that can be corked or otherwise sealed. Plant the two seeds in separate pots or plant them in the ground a foot or more apart. Fill the clear glass container with the spring water, and take it into the sunlight. Feel the earth and its plants growing around you, and amplify this energy with your own vital essence. Direct the energy into the spring water, imparting it with a vibration of amplification and growth. Point your arm or wand toward the sun and draw the sunlight straight down into your body. Bring the energy into your core, feeling it pulsate vibrantly. Amplify this as much as you can, and thinking of it as the essence of pure light, direct the energy back out through your arm and out your fingertip or wand, directly into the water. If all went well, you've now made growth potion. Pour the water into the green container and seal it. Now each time you water the seeds, put a few drops of the growth potion (along with an adequate amount of plain water) on only one of the plants, giving the other plant just the plain water. Notice how the plants grow and see for yourself whether or not your potion making is in tip-top shape.

To customize this practice into an exercise to sharpen your skills, try making different potions to test. For example, you could make a lunar growth potion and try that instead, or you could try adding more ingredients to the solar brewed potion. Or you might create potions of different varieties and dip a similar-looking stone into each one. Then mix up the stones and see if you can tell them apart by touch, sensing whether or not the stone has picked up the energies of the potion.

Protective Power Test

This exercise tests your ability in casting defensive and protective charms. You'll need some cookies for the experiment. Cast your very best protective or defensive charm around one of the cookies, using whatever tools and methods work best for you. Now hold the cookie about five feet above the floor and drop it. Did your protection hold, or did the cookie crumble?

You can vary this exercise by trying different protective spells or charms on a number of cookies and seeing which one works best.

Herb Magick Challenge

Here's a way to practice and gauge your working knowledge of herb magick. Go to your kitchen cabinets right now and pull out anything that could be used as a magickal ingredient. Now look outside in your yard and gather a small sample of anything you could use magickally. Your ingredients gathered and spread out before you, sit down with a pen and a piece of paper and brainstorm potions, powders, and other things you could make with whatever you have. Create as many different formulas as possible, just writing down basic recipes based on your knowledge of each plant's unique energies and attributes. To start, you can have handy books for reference, and then when you're ready, remove the books to see if you remember what you're learning.

Herbology Class

I'm the first to say we should develop our own interests and focus on the skills that matter most to us personally. That being said, I must state plainly that every witch should know herbology. It's not necessary to devote the time and energy into the study required to be a master herbalist, but every witch can benefit from having a working knowledge of basic magickal plants and their powers. A good deal of the power that makes all magick happen comes directly from the earth and its biosphere. Plants are of course an essential aspect of that biosphere, and knowing about their magickal potentials can prove very useful in your spellcraft.

Designing your own herbology class is a great way to build your current level of knowledge. Herbology is one of those arts we can never know everything about; even those witches whose gardens inspire envy can challenge themselves to get even better. You should customize your course to suit your convenience and your current knowledge of the subject. Make it challenging, but not so much so that it's overwhelming.

You could focus on learning more about the attributes of plants commonly used in magick, and then study up on how these plants are grown and cared for. Try growing a few. Take it further and learn about organic fertilizers and plant foods that are good for your particular plants, and learn how to propagate those plants, how to properly clip them, how to replant them without damaging the roots, how to use natural pesticides, etc.

Use magick in your magickal garden, too. You might place empowered stones and element-invoking talismans in the dirt, or summon deities or other natural forces to help the garden thrive. You might choose to visit your garden at a certain time each day, water the plants, and then connect with and amplify the vital energy in each plant. Do whatever you like to do to rev up the magick in your garden.

In addition to plant care, your herbology course should include the steady pursuit of new knowledge about plants and their properties. If you don't know the basics, study up on those before heading into exotic plant territory. If you've already got a decent working knowledge of common magickal plants, discover rare botanicals by visiting local gardens and natural areas. If you're stuck in the middle of a city of concrete, visit college botany program websites, state garden websites, and other Internet resources for information about recent scientific discoveries in the wild world of plants.

Studying the Stars

A working knowledge of basic astronomy and astrology is an asset valued by many witches, and with good reason. Planning our magick and our daily doings in line with the planets and stars makes things run more smoothly and gives us insight into the outer cycles and inner workings of the universe we live in. Also, for those who honor equinoxes and solstices, knowing what is actually going on at these times astronomically opens up a world of magickal possibilities.

Take your study of both astronomy and astrology to your own level of interest. You might find that learning the basics of astrology is enough to give you an edge. Being able to at least cast your own horoscope and forecast accurately is enough to go on for many witches, and doesn't take too much time or effort to learn. Other witches find the art fascinating, and take their studies into astrology's deepest complexities.

Astronomy is the same—some may find it an amazing study, while others will be content with a working understanding of basic planetary movements and the orbit of the earth in relation to the sun and moon. At the least, a witch who practices the craft in line with lunar phases and seasonal shifts should be able to explain astronomical basics. The natural witch should know off hand, for instance, the phases of the moon and why it appears that way from earth, and understand also the position of the earth in relation to the sun on each equinox and solstice. Take it as far as you like, and use what you learn to make your magick out of this world.

Witching School

It's up to you to decide how much about magick you need and want to know, and it's up to you to put in the practice and gather the resources and information you need to help you in your studies. Active learning has its payoffs. You'll find your magickal practice invigorated, and you'll be motivated to continue even further on your quest with each new discovery and every triumph. So hit the books, the garden, your cupboards, wherever you need to go and whatever you need to do, and start furthering your witchy education. Your magickal future is in your hands.

EXERCISE

1. Can you think of a way you could test your healing magick skills?
2. What's a magickal skill you would like to improve?
3. What are you currently best at, magickally?
4. How committed are you to furthering your magickal education? What benefits will you gain by learning all you can?
5. How can you use your knowledge of your magickal strengths to customize your spellwork more effectively?

Taking It Further

Of all the magickal skills, techniques, and topics, which would you most like to master? Pick one or two magickal subjects you're willing to focus on and learn more about. Buy books on subjects that interest you and set aside time to study, even as little as twenty minutes a week. If there are basics you never took time to learn or you've gotten rusty at, spend at least five to ten minutes a day on remedial magick lessons until you catch up to where you feel you should be. Brainstorm ways to test your magickal abilities and do your best to track the progress you're making. You'll soon have a record of your travels along your own road to magickal mastery!

23

Meet Your Destiny

You've come a long way on your journey, and you know how to practice magick successfully. It's time to take the next step into total spellcasting fulfillment and embrace your ultimate niche in the world of magick. Are you ready to discover your higher magickal purpose, develop your own style, and take your true place among the mystics? Well, look sharp! You're about to meet and greet your one-of-a-kind magickal destiny.

Miraculous Magick and Magickal You

While using magick to improve our finances, strengthen our relationships, and make our homes more peaceful are all practical and worthy endeavors, magick is meant for more marvelous miracles, as well. There's a reason you took that first step into the world of magick.

There's a reason you were drawn to reading this particular book. It's time to really take your magickal power by the horns and run with it.

You are unique, and there's a unique purpose to your magickal gifts. It's up to you to find out what that purpose is, and fulfill it. Doing so is truly what constitutes the path—it is your own path toward becoming who you really are and all you can be. It is your path toward using your magickal power to heal the world and improving reality in whatever way only you can. So what will you do? It's time to discover who you *really* are magickally, and decide just what you're going to do about it.

Your Highest Magickal Purpose

Answer these questions and contemplate until you're able to state in one sentence exactly what your highest magickal purpose is as an individual who is gifted with inherent power to change reality.

- Who or what in this world do you most want to help, and what would you like to provide?

- What are your magickal strengths?

- To what sort of magickal goals are you most often drawn?

- If you could magickally accomplish absolutely anything, what would it be? Can you do this? Why or why not?

- Imagine describing yourself to somebody, not as you are now, but as your most ideal and mystical self, the you that you want to become. What details does the description include?

- In what ways do you hope the world will be affected by your life? What can you do to make sure that happens?

- Who are you, as a unique spiritual entity? How is your energy pattern special? What can you do that no one else can do?

- Borrow from Christianity for a moment and imagine yourself in the midst of an apocalyptic scene of death and disaster. It's your job to save humanity from destruction and mayhem. What do you see yourself doing in this situation, imagining yourself having all magickal power at your fingertips and at your command?

• What is your highest magickal purpose that you hope to fulfill?

Meditate on these questions. Ask your deities or higher powers for guidance. Use divination to seek for answers. You can always refine your ideas along the way. The important thing is to get started, because when we do big magick for big things, it never gets dull. Practice your magick, show who you are, and go for it!

Meet Your Destiny Exercise

Try this exercise to help discover your ultimate niche in the world of magick, your own highest destiny. Write down on a piece of paper a statement communicating that you intend to meditate and that you are hoping to receive visions of your ultimate highest destiny. Contact any deities, spirits, or other forces you typically work with, if any. Sit back and close your eyes. Envision yourself hurtling forward through black space in a rush to meet your ultimate self. You might receive visions along the way, or you might just experience the darkness until you find yourself abruptly stopped and standing in front of a vision of the ultimate you in full force. When you come out of the vision, make a sketch of any impressions. Even if your drawing skills aren't exactly great, your pictures will help you remember and bring into manifestation your idea of your ultimate self living your highest destiny.

A Magickal Style All Your Own

We each have our own flavor of magick, and as we bring out this flavor to perfection, our spellwork really gets cooking. So what's your style? Who are you? What do you like? What are you good at? What do you want to do most of all with your magick? Answering these questions helps lead you to a style of magick that suits you, then you can tweak, customize, and refine that style to make it more personal and powerful, a magickal style that is all your own.

Some prefer very traditional magick, while others like contemporary. Some like very structured, complex spells, while others prefer to charm quickly and simply. One witch might dedicate her powers toward healing the sick, while another might use his powers to take out logging machinery.

My own magickal style, to give another example, is that I'm a folky witch with folky leanings and above average abilities in binding and defensive magick. I'm earthy and my magick is mostly light, bright, and practical, though I personally have no qualms about using darker forms of magick for positive ends. It's my magickal mission to encourage more people to put all this good magick we're doing to use on a grander scale. It's my magickal work to help protect and heal the environment and also to defend dogs who are currently being abused and help them escape.

So how does your mission statement go? What is your magickal style, and how can you make that style even more reflective of your own uniqueness? If you're not sure, explore by checking out local groups, books, and websites to see where your interests might lie. Talking to other people involved in magick or Paganism is a great way to gain new experiences and perspectives. Listening to other people's ideas and evaluating those ideas for ourselves helps us discover and refine our own ideas. Your style and your purpose are yours alone.

Exercise

1. What are some ideas you have about your ultimate magickal purpose?
2. What do you suppose your own highest destiny might be?
3. What's your witching style?
4. Do you think that practicing magick in your own way is more effective than practicing another person's style and methods in precise mimicry? Why or why not?
5. What qualities does an awesome style of magick have? What qualities does a mediocre style of magick have?

Taking It Further

What might you do to get more information to continue in your quest to refine and hone your ultimate magickal style to personal perfection? Would divination or meditation help you? Are more magickal practice and experience called for? What techniques or information might be useful in guiding you toward your highest magickal destiny? Seek, and you'll find; don't seek, and you'll just get bored!

24

Mapping the Road Less Traveled

When you walk a magickal path that no one else has ever traveled, you have to make your own map of preferred routes and favorite pit stops. This chapter will give you the inspiration and information you need to effectively craft your own powerful spells, charms, rituals, and traditions. Develop your own complete system of magick that will keep you out of the rut of spellcasting boredom and mediocrity for good.

Spellcrafting Your Way

Most likely, you've designed plenty of spells over the course of your practice. Are you ready to challenge yourself to craft spells that are even more personalized and effective? Building a spell from the ground up is a lot of fun, and if you want to develop a complete magickal system all your own, you'll need to choose basic spells to incorporate into your personal tradition's body of knowledge. Use the following framework for crafting any type of spell. These are the essentials that must be provided for one way or another. Just how you choose to do that is up to you.

Spellcrafting Framework
Magickal Goal

_____

Magickal Mindset (How will you achieve it?)

_____

Energy Raising (From where will you gather power?)

_____

Energy Coding (How will you code the energy with your intent?)

_____

Energy Release (How will you cast the spell and where will it go?)

_____

For your own magickal tradition, design spells to cover all the basics: healing, protection, defense, wealth, love, mood-lifting, whatever you want to include. Create a signature spell, one that is uniquely you, that you can cast whenever you want to boost your own personal power.

Charm Crafting Your Way
Your unique system of magick should also include a set of standard charms of your own design. You might want to create weather magick charms, defensive charms, transfiguration charms, love charms, and more. It's up to you. Make the charms you design reflect your own style and the style of magick you want to develop. Here's a framework showing the essentials of charm crafting.

Charm Crafting Framework

Power (Will you use only your own power or call on other forces?)

_____

Visualization

_____

Words Used, if any

_____

Charm Casting (How will the charm be released?)

_____

Remember that with a charm, magick's four essentials happen automatically. They are still part of the process.

Ritual Crafting Your Way

Every complete system of magick needs its own rituals. Designing your own very personal rituals in honor and celebration of your unique conceptions of deities or higher powers brings you closer to these forces. Your rituals become more relevant and meaningful when you custom-craft them to fit with our own beliefs. Decide what sort of rituals you would like to include as standbys in your own magickal tradition. You might craft rituals to celebrate the moon, sun, seasons, gods, or the elements You could even create a ritual in honor of nothing more than the act of ritual itself. Here is a framework you can use to give you a starting place in making your own moving and mystical rituals.

Ritual Crafting Framework

Date and Time of Ritual

_____

In Honor or Celebration of

_____

Symbols

_____

Ritual Opening

_____

Offerings

_____

Mysteries Enacted

_____

Spoken Words, if any

_____

Special Traditions

_____

Magickal Workings, if any

_____

Ritual Closing

_____

After-Party, if any

_____

Design at least four annual rituals to include in your own system of magick, and you'll be well on your way to having a full-fledged magickal tradition that's all your own.

Traditions for Your Tradition

There is great power in tradition. Just as certain ancient magicks have behind them the accumulated power of centuries of intention, infusing your own magickal system with traditions, special acts repeated on a regular basis, builds up the power of your magick and enriches your personal craft.

What traditions will you include in your customized magickal system? Did you have any pleasant traditions when you were a kid? If so, what did you enjoy? If not, what did you always dream of having? Could any of these ideas be adapted into rituals or other acts and incorporated into your magickal tradition?

Think of special times and events you might want to commemorate, special anniversaries or dates marking major turning points of fate. Do you have a special tradition in honor of your discovery of magick, or in celebration of your continued journey down your path? Are there special traditions you would like to enjoy on seasonal holidays? Are there lost loved ones who have passed on that you would like to remember on certain days?

Your traditions can be formal or informal, fun or a time of sorrow. You might mark a certain day by playing with a favorite childhood toy or talking to an old imaginary friend. You might enjoy a tradition of sharing a magickal rite with a real friend to celebrate a special memory. You could create spiritual traditions in honor of your dearest deities. What traditions are worthy of inclusion into your own ultimate system of magick?

Switch up your magick and rituals to keep your current of magickal power flowing, but also have some traditional practices to serve as nice little places to rest along your path and see and enjoy how far you've come. Here's a framework to help you design your own magickal and spiritual traditions.

New Traditions Framework
Special Days in My Life

Anniversaries of Spiritual Accomplishments

Anniversaries of Personal Accomplishments

Deities, Magickal Powers, Forces, Nature Aspects I Honor

People, Animals, or Places I Want to Honor

This Tradition Will Commemorate

Mood/Tone of this Tradition

What this Tradition Entails

Special Activities to Include

Special Items to include

Try to create at least a few new traditions, and make your mark on the world of witchery!

Your Own Complete System of Magick

Now all it takes to make your own complete system of magick is to put it all together and keep making it better. Even our own magick gets boring when it's not growing! That's why in addition to your rituals, traditions, and other components of your path, it's vital to have a built-in vehicle for taking you further along in a steady pursuit of greater spiritual, psychic, and magickal development. Let's take a look at the components of an effective, complete, personalized system of magick:

- A style, a theme, a magickal mission, or ultimate purpose
- Body of magick (spells, charms, etc.)
- Rituals
- Traditions
- Spiritual philosophies
- Magickal theories
- Magickal development
- Psychic development
- Spiritual development
- Personalization to reflect your own affinities
- Customization to make maximum use of your own abilities
- A steadily traveled path
- Variety and fun

How will you carry out each component in your own tradition? What will your own system of magick be like?

Magickal Power, Powerful Magick

When our souls are nourished with an ever-present fresh flow of new discoveries and truths around every bend, we grow. When we continuously sharpen and hone our magickal skills, our magick thrives. When we entertain and exercise our psychic sense by using it regularly and creatively, our awareness increases. When we do magick our own way, we give it the true secret of success.

As humans and as practitioners of magick, Nature sustains us and inspires us at such a level that the gratitude we feel cannot be put into words. Let's therefore show our love by taking care of the living energy, the sacred magickal power that courses throughout creation, working to free it where it is trapped, heal it where it is hurt, and protect it from further destruction.

Magickal power is yours. It's in you, and no one else on earth is the same as that particular part of the all that is you. It's up to you alone to fully make good on all the magick with which you were gifted. It's up to you to let your spirit do what it must.

INDEX

RECOMMENDED READING

Blavatsky, H.P. *The Secret Doctrine.* 1877. Reprint. Wheaton, IL: Quest Books, 1993.

Buckland, Ray. *Buckland's Book of Spirit Communications.* St. Paul, MN: Llewellyn Publications, 1993.

———. *Buckland's Complete Book of Witchcraft.* St. Paul, MN: Llewellyn Publications, 1986.

———. *Practical Candleburning Rituals.* 1970. Reprint. St. Paul, MN: Llewellyn Publications, 1996.

Cunningham, Scott. *The Complete Book of Incense, Oils, and Brews.* St. Paul, MN: Llewellyn Publications, 1989.

———. *Cunningham's Encyclopedia of Magical Herbs.* St. Paul, MN: Llewellyn Publications, 1985.

Digitalis, Raven. *Planetary Spells and Rituals.* Woodbury, MN: Llewellyn Publications, 2010.

———. *Shadow Magick Compendium.* Woodbury, MN: Llewellyn Publications, 2008.

Heldstab, Celeste. *The Kitchen Grimoire.* Kearney, NE: Morris Press Cookbooks, 2005.

McKenna, Terence. *Food of the Gods.* New York: Bantam Books, 1992.

Meuninck, Jim. *The Basic Essentials of Edible Wild Plants and Useful Herbs.* Merrillville, IN: ICS Books, 1988.

Ody, Penelope. *The Complete Medicinal Herbal.* New York: Dorling Kindersley, 1993.

Papus. *Tarot of the Bohemians.* 1892. Reprint. Chatsworth, CA: Wilshire Book Company, 1982.

Quinn, Paul. *Tarot for Life.* Wheaton, IL: Quest Books, 2009.

Smith, Emily A. *Anxiety Sucks!* Bloomington, IN: AuthorHouse, 2009.

Waite, Arthur E. *Pictorial Key to the Tarot.* 1911. Reprint. Stamford, CT: U.S. Games Systems, Inc., 1971.

Weschcke, Carl, and Joe H. Slate. *Psychic Empowerment for Everyone.* Woodbury, MN: Llewellyn Publications, 2009.